Five Comedies
of Medieval France

FIVE COMEDIES OF MEDIEVAL FRANCE

Translated and with an Introduction by
Oscar Mandel

UNIVERSITY
PRESS OF
AMERICA

LANHAM • NEW YORK • LONDON

Copyright © 1982 by

University Press of America,® Inc.

4720 Boston Way
Lanham, MD 20706

3 Henrietta Street
London WC2E 8LU England

All rights reserved

Printed in the United States of America

Copyright © 1970 by Oscar Mandel

Library of Congress Cataloging in Publication Data
Main entry under title:

Five comedies of medieval France.

   Reprint.   Originally published: New York : Dutton, 1970.
   Bibliography: p.
   Contents: The comic drama in the Middle Ages / Oscar Mandel — The play of Saint Nicholas / Jean Bodel —[etc.]
The play of Robin and Marion / Adam de la Halle —[etc.]
   1. French drama—To 1500—Translations into English.
2. English drama—Translations from French.   I. Mandel, Oscar.
PQ1342.E5F58   1982   842'.0523'08   82-13499
ISBN 0-8191-2668-3 (pbk.)

CAUTION: Professionals and amateurs are hereby warned that all the plays in this volume, being fully protected under the copyright laws of the United States of America, the British Commonwealth, including the Dominion of Canada, and all other countries of the Berne and Universal Copyright Conventions, are subject to royalty. All rights of performance under any condition whatsoever are reserved by the author, from whom all permissions to perform any of these plays must be secured in writing.

OSCAR MANDEL was born in Antwerp, Belgium in 1926 and emigrated to the United States in 1940. He took his degrees at New York, Columbia, and Ohio State Universities and is currently Professor of Humanities at the California Institute of Technology. Dr. Mandel's contacts with the world of drama have been many-sided. He is foremost a playwright, with his first volume of *Collected Plays* being published in the fall of 1970. His plays have been staged, broadcast, and televised throughout the United States. Dr. Mandel is also a student and translator of drama: his *Definition of Tragedy* was published in 1961 and followed in 1963 by a critical history of the Don Juan theme with major representative plays published together in his *Theatre of Don Juan*. He is also the translator of *Seven Comedies of Marivaux* (1968) and the author of two books of fantasy, *Chi Po and the Sorcerer* (1964) and *Gobble-Up Stories* (1966), as well as many articles and poems in literary quarterlies.

for Adriana

*ella è quanto de ben pò far natura;
por esemplo di lei bieltà si prove.*

Contents

INTRODUCTION:
The Comic Drama in the Middle Ages   11

JEAN BODEL:
The Play of Saint Nicholas
(*Le Jeu de Saint Nicholas*, ca. 1200)   35

ADAM DE LA HALLE:
The Play of Robin and Marion
(*Le Jeu de Robin et Marion*, ca. 1285)   77

ANONYMOUS:
Peter Quill's Shenanigans
(*La Farce de Maître Pierre Pathelin*, 1485?)   105

ANONYMOUS:
Two Farces—*The Washtub*; *The Chicken-Pie and the Chocolate Cake*
(*Le Cuvier; Le Pâté et la tarte*, 15th century)   139

INTRODUCTION:
The Comic Drama in the Middle Ages

I. Comedy of the Middle Ages has its own character, its own strong points, its own limitations. It can be very funny, it is rapid and peppery, but we had better not look to it for acute psychological insights, penetrating criticism of life, philosophical reverberations, or even witty repartee in our sense of the expression. The greatest writers did not write for the stage. Drama was clearly less prestigious than the epic or lyric forms. Even when serious, it was popular and it avoided subtleties. And yet, here and there, something very much like genius winks at us from both the serious and the comic drama of these centuries. And in the fifteenth century genuine masterpieces begin to multiply. Even in these, however, comedy remains farcical or, at any rate, "insignificant." What saves it is that when insignificance shows itself off at its best, it acquires an unexpected solidity. Men refuse to forget it. Manuscripts multiply. The presses deliver copies. And centuries later we realize that the precious things of life lie, high and low, all along the gamut of the human repertory.

What kinds of dramatic comedy do we encounter in the Middle Ages? First of all, the entirely secular farce. Second, the religious play that has been turned into comedy or farce, or that has a farce embedded in it. Third, the farce disguised as a morality play. Fourth, the satirical revue in which the Fool and his associates satirize church, state, and individuals, usually without a clear plot. And fifth, the humorous eclogue or pastoral. In the present volume, the reader will find three secular farces, a humorous miracle play, and a musical pastoral.

The beginnings are all but lost to us. In the sixth century of our era the Roman theatre became extinct, and the mimes who had entertained Rome's motley populace with low farces and satires dispersed. The Dark Ages follow. Perhaps they are darker to us for want of records than they were for the dwellers of field, castle, monastery, and town. For life persisted, as it doggedly does when empires die, and so did most of the diversions necessary to sustain it. The mimes were now bereft of theatres, but not of the will to make theatre. We watch them through the words of lawmakers, theologians, moralists, and historians from one end of Europe to the other. They went under a variety of names, some flattering, others invidious. Here, for the sake of convenience, I shall call them *minstrels* and forgo finer discriminations.

These minstrels sang ditties, chanted or recited wonderful tales—long and short, heroic, domestic, pious, or bawdy—mimed and danced, showed off animals or puppets, juggled, tumbled, performed tricks, impersonated their betters, hid their faces behind masks; in short, they provided art, entertainment, and even edification for the public in exchange for the wherewithal to live. Lords and ladies received them gladly in great halls. Villagers surrounded them in the market place. And monks were happy to feed and lodge them for the sake of a story and a song. They traveled light. Any place out of the rain was a possible stage. Some were poor rogues, but some became councillors to kings. A few had genius and proclaimed the important difference between a creator (a *trouvère*, a finder) and a lowly *joculator* or juggler. Many knew how to compose a tale, a ballad, or a song. Far more, we can be sure, sang with bad voices, played a mediocre lute, and had no ideas. But they were all professionals, and, scarcely differentiated then in fact, by law or in the public mind, they were destined to evolve and branch out to make a host of modern specialists like poets, actors, composers, musicians, stagehands, acrobats, directors, dancers, and twenty or thirty other species of artist-entertainers.

The question that poses itself for us is whether these minstrels also performed what we now call plays. We are in the seventh, the eighth, the ninth century—have the minstrels forgotten what it is to exchange words (or blows!) as if they were no longer minstrels but villagers or merchants or churchmen? We hear of farces in Byzantium—but what of France, Germany, Italy, England? No texts subsist, and as for bishops who fulminated against mimes and others who defended them, or laws that sought to curb their excesses, we cannot tell whether they refer to monologues, pantomimes, or genuine drama.

But here it is well to remember that the distinction between dramatic and narrative literature, which seems essential to us, had virtually no significance in the centuries of oral delivery. A minstrel would give an "impassioned performance" of something we should call today a short story or a novella. He recited or chanted a tale of war or love with an actor's gestures and modulations. In passages of dialogue—they were frequent —he changed his voice in an appropriate manner. On other occasions he omitted narration altogether, and impersonated a huckster or a friar. He would go even further, and again without narration he would enact a debate—say, between the body and the soul, or (for another audience) between a seducer and a farm girl. Is this theatre or not? Let us suppose that he was joined in his story or debate by a fellow minstrel. The modern scholar cries out, "Here at last is true theatre," but neither the minstrels nor their audiences would have felt the leap into a new category. For them, passing from recitation to monologue, and from monologue to duologue, would be "all in the day's work." To narrate a fabliau or to perform a skit was to fish in the same pool. They could not foresee that time would keep widening the difference, that printing would act as a great divider, until all men would feel the need for separate names: the novel here, and the drama there.

Even without surviving texts, and even forgetting the origins of minstrelsy in the Roman theatre, we can be fairly confident that throughout the Dark Ages, into the Middle Ages, and up to the fifteenth century when texts begin to abound, the art of the minstrel included the performance of simple skits. If not, the omission would have to be explained, for it would be extremely puzzling. Why on earth would minstrels *never* do "funny bits" together? It would have to be shown that they always traveled alone, and avoided contact with each other in town and countryside. And what would we make of the art of puppetry, which is amply documented for the twelfth century? Were the puppeteers inventing skits independently of ordinary minstrels? This is most unlikely. Whenever and wherever men have made puppets perform, they have imitated the materials of the "real" theatre. In the twelfth century, and most probably long before, these materials must have come from the "pitiable farce," as E. K. Chambers has called it, of street and market place. Finally, when, in the thirteenth century, our first texts emerge, they are seen to belong to the ancient Roman family in personage and subject matter. A tradition which had never died out was now allowing history a first glimpse into its domain.

But how shall we explain the absence of early texts? Of course it comes as no surprise that there are fewer records for the eighth than for the thirteenth century. But we may well ask how many manuscripts existed to begin with. In his *Origini della poesia drammatica italiana*, Vicenzo de Bartholomaeis argues convincingly that these skits were seldom if ever put down at all. The routines of gags, simple tricks, and coarse clowning were performed extemporaneously—as with the later *commedia dell'arte* or the famous clowns of sixteenth- and seventeenth-century Paris—because they were simple to remember, easy to imitate, and no trouble to pass on to another generation. By contrast, individual minstrels composing and then reciting long tales were normally obliged to commit them to writing. Such manuscripts were precious, occasionally recopied, and carefully handed down from one generation of minstrels to the next.

Furthermore, in an age when the art of writing was largely in the hands of churchmen, we would hardly expect these playlets, a good number of which were offensive to the cloth, to find many clerks willing to record them on parchment for posterity. To write down the text of a miserable and cynical farce of cuckolds, thieves, and adulterous priests would have seemed as outlandish an idea as would be—for slightly different reasons—the idea today of a professor giving a course in the literature of the television commercial. In this connection, an instructive parallel comes to us from thirteenth-century Italy. It was the custom there to substitute the words of pious hymns (*lauds*) for the texts of profane songs in order to take advantage of popular tunes. Remarkably, almost none of the lay lyrics survive. No one bothered to preserve them. Yet nearly two hundred *books* of edifying lauds have come down to us, carefully kept, copied, and transmitted by the serious confraternities that had begotten them.

The earliest surviving comic texts come to us as religious plays (which I will be discussing presently) or as elements in religious plays. Perhaps the scribes, taking in hand the dignified task of copying a respectable play, could then innocently smuggle in the low comedy as well. To pursue our analogy, a course in the television commercial would be disgracefully undignified, but a few jingles could certainly be glossed ex cathedra in a context of authorized contemporary literature.

It is also significant that when the texts of farces begin to appear in quantity, namely in the fifteenth century, the art of the farce was no longer largely in the hands of minstrels, but was being enthusiastically taken up by students and citizens, all amateurs who would be in greater need of texts than the professional entertainers.

In any event, the farce reached its maturity in the half century before 1500, growing no doubt with the rise of urban centers. A reading public was developing for them. New farces were being invented and written down. The genre was gaining enough respectability so that prominent men of letters no longer scorned to try their hand at a skit or two. The masterpiece of the genre, *Pathelin*, was clearly the product of an educated man; and it became one of the earliest books to be printed.

Not that the farce came to an end with *Pathelin*. The broad and obstinately "unimportant" skit refused to die out or to alter its complexion on the mere ground that the Middle Ages, according to erudition, had given way to the Renaissance. In the sixteenth century, excellent farces were written by Gil Vicente, Ruzzante, John Heywood, and Hans Sachs, to name only these. At the same time, the *commedia dell'arte* troupes perpetuated the farce in their own manner—more faithfully, in a sense, than anyone else, for they maintained the minstrels' extempore tradition, relying on familiar routines brilliantly executed rather than on fixed scripts. Cervantes published his unrivaled *entremeses* in 1615. In France the tradition of unwritten farce reached Molière, and animated the eighteenth-century open theatres of the fairground (the *théâtres de la foire*). Farce persisted even longer in the German-speaking world, and men were still fighting to preserve the folk theatre of Hans Wurst in nineteenth-century Austria.

Throughout these epochs, strolling amiably across "Dark Ages," "Middle Ages," "Renaissance," and "Enlightenment," the farce remained true to its own little cosmos. Here were the dependable shrewish wives, the cuckolds, the hungry beggars, the boastful cowards, the snippy servants, the impotent octogenarians, the dupes, and the tricksters, all brawling on stage to the accompaniment of blows and farts, insults and groans, shouts and grimaces; then a song and a dance, and money in the hat. In the darkest recesses of the Dark Ages, minstrels would have known better than to forget these profitable routines. And they would have recognized with a start, in an eighteenth-century Bavarian market place, the very gags they had used ten centuries before.

II. The absence of a clear distinction between narration and drama in the Middle Ages can be illustrated in a group of profane comical works in Latin composed in the second half of the twelfth century. These are tales of love, lust, and trickery, some under a hundred lines, and none over eight hundred lines long, written by schoolmasters, advanced students, and perhaps some wandering scholars for classroom use or student entertainment. Most if not all of these pieces are associated with the region of the Loire.[1]

The tales are heavily—and sometimes boastfully—indebted to Menander, Plautus, Terence, and Ovid. Thus the *Geta* retells the classical story of Amphitryon; in the *Alda* a young man enjoys the girl he desires by disguising himself as his own sister; in the *Babio* an old dodderer is cheated of a young girl by her soldier-lover and of his own wife by his servant; and in the *Pamphilus* Venus and an old bawd bring two lovers to bed. The figures of the rascally dumb and rascally clever servants are conspicuous. One servant swallows a fish bone and almost chokes on it; another gets his hands on a large meat pie; a third drubs his master and empties a chamber pot over his head. As for the lovers, the joys of copulation are lusciously described, and now and then enacted, so to speak, before our eyes. Only the romantic Menandrian element of the long-lost daughter or son recognized by an aging parent is missing. Not romance, but rough play and quick sex interested the lads who wrote, read, or acted in these tales.

Two of the Latin pieces—the *Babio* and the extremely brief *De clericis et rustico*—must be called plays, for they are written entirely in dialogue. This has led several scholars, Gustave Cohen among them, to suggest, though cautiously, that we might be in the presence of a genuine school-drama. But the evidence is all against this hypothesis. A highly suggestive range, from almost pure narration to pure drama, meets the

[1] They have been conveniently collected under the supervision of Gustave Cohen (see the bibliography), and translated into French. Unlike the street-corner farce, they "deserved" to be written down because scholars had composed them, and because they claimed descent from the classics.

18   FIVE COMEDIES OF MEDIEVAL FRANCE

eye in this bloc of literature. Some of the pieces are *almost* entirely dramatic. Thus, in the seven hunded and eighty lines of the *Pamphilus* there is but a single "Then Venus told him" to disturb the dialogue. Next to this we see a couple of monologues. For example, in a brief and wretched piece entitled *De tribus sociis*, the speaker tells us how he took revenge on a suspicious pottery merchant by breaking two of his jugs. The other compositions, however, are narratives more or less generously charged with dialogue.

The picture is easy to reconstruct. All the compositions were undoubtedly delivered aloud, whether in the classroom or for entertainment after class. Where we find a great deal of narration, we visualize a student or master taking the narrative part, while others read the several roles. Certain pieces were spoken by one man alone, with suitable changes of voice. Others, like the *Babio*, being all dialogue, required no narrator at all. It is hard to believe that the young scholars announced a narrative on one occasion and a play on another. Whether one of them began a speech with "Then Venus told him" or simply uttered the speech itself could not have mattered very much. Nor is it a momentous problem whether the reciters gesticulated as if impersonating the characters. Bawdy as these stories are, we can assume that the students did not, as the actors of our times do, simulate the sexual intercourse they narrated. We are in a fluid world here, where the performers would pass innocently from narration to impersonation and then back to narration without ever creating a theatre.

For about this there can be no question. Lively as these performances—or *dramatic readings*, as we would call them today —surely were, they leave us in a mere eddy off the main stream of the European theatre. Not until the Renaissance would Europe see a genuine and influential school-drama. At most, we can surmise that whenever we come across a particularly farcical bit in these Latin pieces for which there is no precedent in the Plautine and Terentian drama (the choking on a fish bone? the stolen meat pie?), we might be catching on the rebound a minstrel skit, a fairground farce, overheard and remembered by a clerk who was inditing a "comedy" after Plautus.

III. For a far more important comic vein than the schoolhouse could offer, we turn our eyes to another sector altogether. Independent of minstrel farce, independent of pseudo-antique school-comedy, independent of Rome and Athens, the church had stumbled on a species of drama in the tenth century tailored to its own needs—drama that was as remote as possible from comedy when it was born, but that comedy was quick to invade.

A great deal more is known about this liturgical drama than about the secular skits I have discussed so far, and, for reasons already made plain, an incomparably greater number of texts have survived. Thus we know that in the tenth century, churchmen had taken to enacting with great solemnity, during the Easter morning service, the discovery of the empty sepulcher by the three Marys. The express purpose of dramatizing the rising of Christ was to encourage the congregation's attention. This ceremonial drama, which could not have lasted more than a few minutes, is described as follows by Ethelwold, Bishop of Winchester, around the year 970:

> While the third lesson is being chanted, let four brethren vest themselves. Let one of these, vested in an alb, enter as though to take part in the service, and let him approach the sepulcher without attracting attention and sit there quietly with a palm in his hand. While the third respond is chanted, let the remaining three follow, and let them all, vested in copes, bearing in their hands thuribles with incense, and stepping delicately as those who seek something, approach the sepulcher. These things are done in imitation of the angel sitting in the monument and the women with spices coming to anoint the body of Jesus. When therefore he who sits there beholds

the three approach him like folk lost and seeking something, let him begin in a dulcet voice of medium pitch to sing *Quem quaeritis* [Whom do you seek?]. And when he has sung it to the end, let the three reply in unison *Ihesu Nazarenum*. So he, *Non est hic, surrexit sicut praedixerat* [He is not here, he is risen as he foretold]. *Ite, nuntiate quia surrexit a mortuis* [Go, announce that he is risen from the dead]. At the word of this bidding let those three turn to the choir and say *Alleluia! resurrexit Dominus!* This said, let the one still sitting there and as if recalling them say the anthem *Venite et videte locum* [Come and see the place]. And saying this, let him rise, and lift the veil, and show them the place bare of the cross, but only the cloths laid there in which the cross was wrapped. And when they have seen this, let them set down the thuribles which they bare in the same sepulcher, and take the cloth, and hold it up in the face of the clergy, and as if to demonstrate that the Lord has risen and is no longer wrapped therein, let them sing the anthem *Surrexit Dominus de sepulchro*, and lay the cloth upon the altar. When the anthem is done, let the prior, sharing in their gladness at the triumph of our King, in that, having vanquished death, He rose again, begin the hymn *Te Deum laudamus*. And this begun, let the bells chime together. [2]

Let us briefly note the characteristics of this liturgical play: it is sung, not spoken; its language is Latin; the actors are men of the church; the purpose may be summarized in the familiar phrase, "to instruct by pleasing"; the audience consists of other clergymen, choirboys, and congregation; the mood is solemn yet festive; costumes and props are already in evidence; stage directions are given; and the theatre, of course, is the church itself. We must not omit the observation that here, presiding

[2] Quoted in E. K. Chambers, *Mediaeval Stage* (Oxford, 1903), II, pp. 14–15. For other early specimens, see Joseph Quincy Adams' *Chief Pre-Shakespearean Dramas* (Boston, 1924).

as it were over the creation of modern drama, was that arch-enemy of the stage itself, the Roman Catholic Church, whose spokesmen never tired of blasting the *spectacula inhonesta*, the *spectacula obscoena*, or the *histrionum obscoenas jocationes*.

The originator of the *Quem quaeritis* playlet was probably a monk who dwelled in the monastery of St. Gall, now in northern Switzerland. The name of a certain Tutilo has been proposed. But it has also been suggested that the original notion of "free-lancing" additions to a liturgical text had been carried eastward from France, beset at that time by the invading Norsemen. Whatever the origins, it should be emphasized once more that the monk's invention required no miraculous leap of the imagination. The church ritual was dramatic enough in itself. Moreover, the additions I have just mentioned—they were called *tropes*—sometimes consisted in a dialogue of chants embellishing various portions of the service. Consequently, the next step, that of putting the embellishments into the mouths, not of mere choristers, but of men who pretended to be the very angel or Mary whose words were being sung—the step from reporting to enacting—was impressive, but not astounding. As for the question whether the monk's familiarity with the lively art of the minstrel contributed to his idea, we shall never know the answer to it—but has not the church often helped itself to worldly customs for its godly purposes? We take the slope of nature itself if we suppose that the originator of the Easter representation was simply struck with the idea of appropriating the successful—the all-too successful!—mimicry of the minstrels for the greater glory of God. Perhaps he meant to counteract the bawdy farce by offering a worthy substitute. But this is sheer speculation. No document exists that could turn it into fact.

And yet how else shall we explain that a century or so after the Easter plays were born, they married themselves off to farce and folk custom? At first the bare, austere Easter drama spreads over much of Europe; but presently, somewhat equivocal scenes are added to it. A race between Peter and

John to see who shall be the first to arrive at the empty tomb appears, and we are told that it derives from pre-Christian Germanic games. Next comes a spice merchant who hawks his goods in a comical way and makes a sale when the Marys pass by. Inevitably the merchant acquires a shrewish wife who cuckolds him. Roman soldiers make an entrance to guard the tomb—arrogant and cowardly, like those of the Roman farce and certain minstrel monologues. Plainly these and other ideas penetrate from the outside world; so plainly that the more serious-minded priests begin to register shock. Do these additions derive from minstrel monologues or goliardic poems, or are they not rather inspired by the secular skits—vestiges of the Roman farce—whose omnipresence I have postulated?

The story of how the vast and colorful garden of medieval drama grew out of the seed sown at St. Gall can be summarized here in a few words. The church quickly grasped the possibility of dramatizing other vital portions of sacred history at various times of the year. Soon, too, Latin yielded to the vernacular and chant to speech. A good deal of profane merriment attached itself, as we have seen, to the edifying action. The entire business grew too complicated, time-consuming, and worldly for the clergy to handle by itself, and in many places the *mysteries*, as the plays dealing with Old and New Testament matter were called, were gradually taken over by guilds of lay citizens—all amateurs, of course—who carried the plays out of the church into the market place, the street, the guildhall, and occasionally to a noble private house.

By the fourteenth and fifteenth centuries vast performances lasting several days and sometimes involving hundreds and even thousands of citizens were being given in many parts of Europe. Nothing less than the history of the universe from the creation to the Last Judgment was exhibited to the public view at these times, with the Passion of Christ at the center of the events. And yet it also happened that in other places a conservative tendency prevailed. Although the liturgical texts were growing more elaborate, more amusing, more worldly, and less manageable, in many dioceses the priests continued to use the ancient Latin trope virtually as in the beginning.

Miracle plays—plays dealing with the lives of saints—appeared perhaps within a century of the earliest Easter drama. Like the latter, they were probably a monastic invention, originating at the confluence of several forces: the importance of saints and their miracles in the medieval world, countless celebrations of saints' days, study of the lives and miracles of saints in schools and monasteries, frequent appearances of minstrels who, when they performed for monks or nuns, exchanged their bawdy stories for instructive or pseudo-instructive tales of saints, and above all the example of the highly successful liturgical drama. It would be strange indeed if the mystery play had not grown to include the miracles that testified to the faith. For that matter, the distinction between the two classes of religious drama quickly became a tenuous one. The most popular subject of miracle plays was Our Lady herself. Here the personage belongs to the mystery, the actions to the miracle. If we add to this that the miracle underwent the same development as the strictly liturgical play, from Latin to the vernacular, from church to guildhall, from earnest piety to comedy, we may be inclined to drop the distinction altogether in favor of a general idea of the religious drama in the Middle Ages.

It stands to reason that the more firmly the laity took hold of dramatic productions, the greater was the temptation to borrow ideas from the minstrels. A fundamental shift takes place: religion yields to art, salvation to aesthetic satisfaction, edification to entertainment—three ways of saying the same thing. The Easter trope could never have become "art" in any legitimate sense of the word had not the purpose of giving pleasure (whether by a serious or a comic action) unobtrusively outdistanced the purpose of improving the mind. And if entertainment—often outright comedy—could be smuggled into matters like the Flood, the Massacre of the Innocents, the Crucifixion, and the Last Judgment, how could the lives of saints resist? Here the stories, though unimpeachably true, were less sacrosanct, the imagination less restricted by authority, and the histories themselves often down to earth and easily fitted into contemporary settings. As a result, many miracles are little more than a pretext for a fabulous tale, serious, romantic, comical, or all three, in which the Virgin or another saint functions as a last-minute *deus ex machina*. In France, the most famous specimen of the comic miracle is Jean Bodel's *Jeu de Saint Nicolas*, translated in this volume. It bears the early date of 1200, and is already a full-blown comedy. In the fourteenth century, the very titles of certain miracles—*Berthe aux grands pieds, Amis et Amile, La Fille du roi de Hongrie*—tell us how far we have moved from the early liturgical drama.

When, in the fifteenth century, the *morality* became a popular genre—*Everyman* is the best-known example—it too swiftly moved from edification to amusement. Characters like Faith or Good Conscience are jostled by personages named Nought, New-Guise, and Nowadays, or, in France, Colicque, Gourmandise, Rien, and Tardive-à-bien-faire. A group of players—by now some of them are full-time, professional actors rather than unspecialized minstrels—could announce a morality with a respectable title, and then produce a farce in which Abstractions behaved no better than the Mimin and the Thévot of the regular farce.

In sum, a few generations after the birth of the liturgical drama, the wandering minstrels had lost their monopoly over comedy. The mystery, the miracle, and later the morality, all in the hands of amateur performers, had opened themselves to farce, and it is a fair guess that the latter was better nourished in these respectable mansions than on the open road. The clerks and bards who composed these pious or pseudo-pious pieces drew not only on the repertory of the professional clowns of the market place, but also on a large mass of written literature of racy stories and bohemian verse. They were men of letters; with them the comic spirit such as we meet it in Bodel's play or in the English *Second Shepherds'*

Pageant became far more sophisticated than what a tenth-century audience could expect from its minstrels. We can think of the religious drama of the Middle Ages as a kind of acceleration chamber in which the rudimentary early farce received a powerful boost.

This much said, it must not be forgotten that many religious plays moved from Latin to the vernacular, and from church to city, without absorbing any comic elements. The picture is fluid. We cannot separate medieval religious drama into comic and serious compartments. The question is *how* comic, *how* serious is the action? Some texts are almost pure farce, with an edifying miracle hastily worked up at the end; but many others are entirely elevated and serious. Elevated and serious, for—to digress a moment—we can seldom speak of *tragic* drama in the Middle Ages. The serious mysteries, miracles, and moralities stress the hopeful side of Christianity. He who comes to a bad end deserved to come to a bad end. Conversely, if a man is good, he will come to good in the end. And if he was bad in the beginning, but repented in time, God will take him to His bosom. Great and passionate conflicts of the mind, tragic renunciations, victories of evil are beyond even the best of these plays, which can do no more than flash off hints of tragedy, fugitive moments of destructive anguish. For the medieval drama remained obstinately popular; what mattered above all was a great bustle.[3]

IV. Much of the dramatic activity I have been describing was open to the general public. The average citizen, if he was not himself playing Herod or a Roman soldier, could watch a

[3] A handful of serious *secular* plays, probably performed in literary societies or before noble households, have come down to us; and among them, an interesting Dutch dramatization of a tale of chivalry, *Lancelot of Denmark*, which can properly be called tragic. But the evidence available to us suggests that serious or tragic secular drama, like the Latin school-drama I have mentioned before, is a minor spur off the main literary road.

serious or funny show in church, in a square or a street, or anywhere a group of minstrels might be allowed to set up a stage. The occasion might be Easter, Christmas, Carnival, Corpus Christi day, any saint's day, a patriotic celebration, or the visit of a prince. But certain events were addressed to a more limited group. The Feast of Fools, for example, was a partly dramatic revel organized by the cathedral's functionaries for their own solace. The inferior clergy were allowed once a year to burlesque their betters and to parody holy texts and rites. Like the Carnival, this saturnalian event belongs only marginally to our subject. A much more important phenomenon was the development of literary societies (called *puys* in France), where, among other activities, the members indulged in amateur theatricals. The repertory consisted of standard mysteries, miracles, moralities, and farces, but certain kinds of drama, like the familiar topical satirical revue and the serious secular play, appear to have been created within these societies. Reputable minstrels were active members of the *puys*. Here too, therefore, we can speak of both a qualitative and a quantitative increase in dramatic activity.

By the fifteenth century we encounter throughout France groups of citizens, and especially groups of students, banded in what we would call theatrical clubs whose sole function was to prepare and produce plays. In Paris, one such group seems to have been granted a monopoly over the Passion play, and another over the farce. But the large picture of the Middle Ages shows us these groups performing in addition to the others I have named, and indeed to some I have not—villagers of the kind Shakespeare exhibits in *A Midsummer Night's Dream*, or, for that matter, any citizen who could get a few friends and acquaintances together for a bit of fun in the open. There were no theatrical unions in the Middle Ages and very few official restrictions concerning who could or who could not produce a farce or a morality. Hence a certain confusion for the neat historian, but a colorful confusion suggesting a wide choice for the medieval lover of drama. It is plain, at any rate, that the tempo of dramatic activity rose throughout the Middle Ages with only a few local setbacks, and that in the fifteenth century theatre flourished as never before. It was still largely in the hands of the amateur public itself, and not until the 1580's would the first permanent professional houses be built in Europe.

Amateur theatricals flourished in the halls of the nobility as well. Plays might be written for any suitable occasion—a birthday, a victory, Christmas, or a banquet. Men like Adam de la Halle and Gil Vicente were household bards who could compose trifles on demand, direct the productions, and perform a part. Much of the entertainment of princes was undoubtedly nondramatic—dance, pantomime, music, narration, *tableaux vivants*—but Adam's *Jeu de Robin et Marion*, translated in the following pages, gives us an idea of how a pastoral, or a chivalric romance, might be adapted to the stage by a clever poet. Very little concrete documentation is available for all the centuries from the Carolingian age, when we know that certain plays were performed before kings, to fifteenth- and sixteenth-century Italy, where great men financed sumptuous entertainments that included dramatic performances of the classics. But when a sophisticated text like *Robin et Marion* surfaces in the thirteenth century without apparently evoking any surprise among contemporaries, we can only conclude that court entertainment of a dramatic kind existed before, and probably long before, the specimen that was recorded and preserved.

V. I have said that no texts remain of the minstrel farce of the Dark Ages and the early Middle Ages. A number of scholars deny that this farce existed at all. For them, theatrical activity becomes extinct with Rome and does not stir again until the *Quem quaeritis* trope is born. At which date, we can now ask, is the existence of a comedy totally independent of the church actually proved? Not, it turns out, before the thirteenth century, when just enough documents emerge to suggest that independent comedy was no rarity. In England we find an *Interludium de clerico et puella* in Northumbrian dialect. In France Adam de la Halle wrote his *Jeu de la Feuillée*, a local satirical skit, in 1276. A decade or two before, Alfonso X, in his renowned compilation of laws, the *Siete Partidas*, had referred unambiguously to *"juegos de escarnio,"* that is to say, farces. However, a French *Le Garçon et l'Aveugle*, from the latter half of the thirteenth century, is our first actual farce in the vernacular. It is followed around 1290 by the knockabout *Jeu du Pèlerin*, a crude but historically valuable curtain-raiser for *Robin et Marion*.

The fourteenth century yields the text of six notable Dutch farces, and a legal text of 1499 in Paris claims that "diffamatory farces," offensive to ecclesiastical authority, have been current in all of Picardy, "and even in Paris," for over two hundred years. Admittedly, however, it is only in the fifteenth century that the texts of farces proliferate, indicating either that the farce suddenly boomed, or that it was now more frequently written down, or that the survival rate for manuscripts became more favorable, or that more copies of manuscripts were being made.

It cannot therefore be proved beyond all possibility of doubt that the genre of the farce survived in the centuries following the destruction of the Roman empire. Indeed, an extreme case can be, and has been, made for the hypothesis that before the fifteenth century any comedy other than that associated with religious drama was a singular event. The following chart, which the reader may find helpful, rests on the contrary assumption that the minstrels never ceased to perform elementary secular skits, and that a *submerged continuity* exists, linking late medieval comedy to Roman ancestors through the antics of wandering entertainers.[4]

---

[4] The chart omits all narrative and nonliterary influences on the drama.

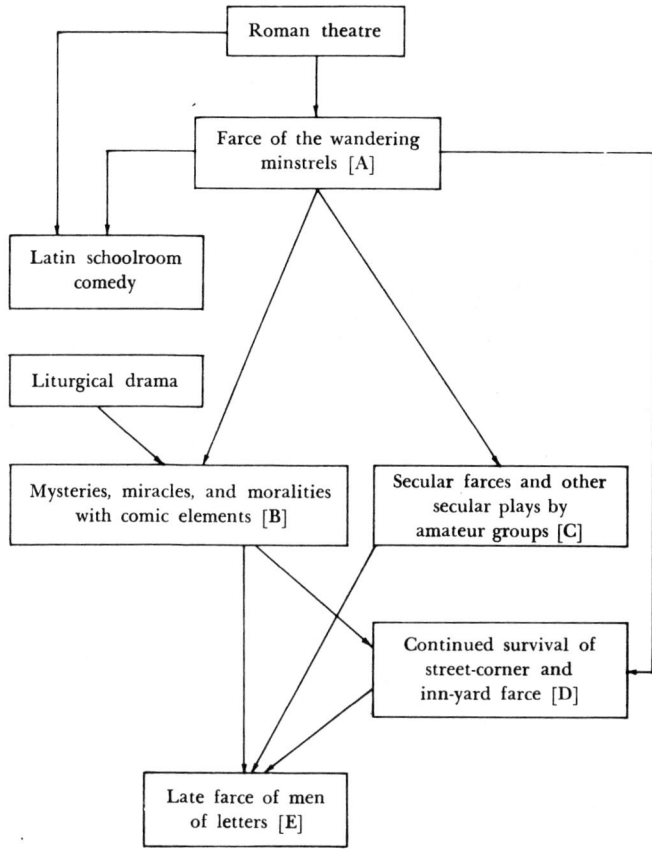

- [A] Earliest surviving example: thirteenth-century *Le Garçon et l'Aveugle*.
- [B] Like *Le Jeu de Saint Nicolas* (thirteenth century).
- [C] Like *Le Jeu de la Feuillée, Robin et Marion* (thirteenth century), and *Pathelin*.
- [D] Like *Le Cuvier* (fifteenth century).
- [E] E.g., Gil Vicente and Hans Sachs.

ABOUT THIS BOOK

As far as I am aware, the present collection is the first of its kind in the English language. My hope is that it will open the door to other and larger collections. Discouragingly few texts of European medieval plays are available in English. Of the rich repertory of French plays, whether light or grave, a minute fraction is offered here. Not a single Italian play of the Middle Ages exists in English. Not a single *Fastnachtspiel*. A few Dutch plays have been translated in single editions, but all are out of print. Needless to say, we possess nothing of the medieval drama of Eastern Europe. Even scholarly works concerning this entire field are rare in English.

Beyond the strict confines of the Middle Ages, and pursuing the farce into later times, we discover four plays by Gil Vicente in our language, one by Ruzzante, nothing by Juan del Encina, nothing by Hans Sachs. Only recently have we had the good fortune to see the best of Cervantes' farces in English through the excellent translations of Edwin Honig.

To return to the pre-Renaissance era, it is to be hoped that a large-scale anthology of medieval drama can be compiled some day, in which the finest European plays in all modes, including the best English plays in actable and readable modern English, will be made available for enjoyment and study. The present collection could occupy one chapter of such an anthology.

The reader of a translated work has the right to know what kind of translation is being presented to him. I have followed the same principles that I laid down in the *Seven Comedies by Marivaux* recently published by my wife and myself. These translations are not for students of the period who require a word-for-word knowledge of the original, whether for historical or linguistic research. I have tried instead to comply with two overriding demands: the first, *to remain absolutely faithful to the conceptual and emotional essence of each semantic unit;* the second, *to naturalize these plays into modern English.* The second of these goals cannot be met unless the translator is free to use words, phrases, allusions, and rhetorical turns of his own time and place. But the first condition sets a strong wall around this freedom. At no time may the translator go beyond the essential meaning and emotion of any given semantic unit for the sake of modernity. For if he does this, he slips into adaptation: the play becomes partly his own.

A moment's thought tells us that if we wish to remain faithful to the emotional essence of an ancient original, we are *compelled* to struggle partly free from it and to naturalize it. We realize, for example, that where the original expressed no anger, we must not put anger in. Where the original expressed no awe, we must not introduce awe. Similarly, however, where the original expressed no feeling of strangeness, we too must leave strangeness out. I am referring, of course, to the strangeness of the archaic, the long-ago, the quaint. As long as we insist on translating a medieval text literally, we are bound to inject this extremely vivid feeling, though it was absent from the original, and thus to lapse unwittingly into adaptation by virtue of excessive faithfulness.

For one instance among a hundred, when Pathelin boasts to his wife that he is a clever lawyer even though he is not a learned man, he says, literally, "I dare boast that I can sing from the missal with our priest as well as if I had gone to school as long as Charles in Spain." The student of history or language will want this passage reproduced precisely as I have done here, but as literature this translation is false. Leaving to one side the question of style, we can assume that the simile taken from church life and the allusion to Charles in Spain were plain and modern to the audience. The "conceptual essence" of the passage requires that we keep the idea of his boast; but the "emotional essence" of the original is devoid of the archaic, and thus we must find a nonarchaic equivalent, literally false but emotionally true.

For the same reason French names are turned into English names, and, for example, Pathelin becomes Peter Quill (or something else). The name "Patterlynn" is odd and foreign to the English or American listener, whereas it is certainly not odd or foreign even to the Frenchman who may never have heard it before. True, there are certain obstacles to rebaptizing characters. If Pathelin were as much a household name for us as, say, Don Quixote, or if the locale of the action were emphatically French, we could not operate our transfer. These obstacles, however, do not exist in any of the plays before us.

No one will expect the translator of these plays to use verse, though the originals do. Although lively, the original verse never soars into poetry. Its function was mnemonic, not aesthetic.

To conclude, the reader can be assured that, in spite of the modern American idiom he is about to encounter, the plays in this volume are not adaptations but genuine translations. And the more modern, the more suitable to the stage they appear to him, the more genuinely they are translated.

BIBLIOGRAPHY

I list the works that have been most helpful to me in preparing the introduction to this book.

D'ANCONA, A. *Origini del teatro italiano.* (2nd ed.), 2 vols. Torino, 1891.

DE BARTHOLOMAEIS, VICENZO. *Origini della poesia drammatica italiana.* (2nd ed.). Torino, 1952.

BÉDIER, JOSEPH. "Commencements du théâtre comique en France." *Revue des Deux Mondes,* Vol. 99 (1890), pp. 869–897.

CHAMBERS, E. K. *The Medieval Stage.* 2 vols. Oxford, 1903.

COHEN, GUSTAVE. *La Comédie latine en France au XIIe siècle.* 2 vols. Paris, 1931.

———. *Le Théâtre en France au moyen âge.* Paris, 1928, 1931.
CRAWFORD, J. P. W. *Spanish Drama Before Lope de Vega.* (rev. ed.). Philadelphia, 1937.
DONOVAN, RICHARD B. *The Liturgical Drama in Medieval Spain.* Toronto, 1958.
FARAL, EDMOND. *Les Jongleurs en France au moyen âge.* Paris, 1909.
FRANK, GRACE. *The Medieval French Drama.* Oxford, 1954.
FRAPPIER, JEAN. *Le Théâtre profane en France au moyen âge.* Paris, 1961.
HÉLIN, MAURICE. *A History of Medieval Latin Literature.* (rev. ed.). Translated by J. C. Snow. New York, 1949.
JACOBSEN, J. P. *Essai sur les origines de la comédie en France au moyen âge.* Paris, 1910.
KINDERMANN, HEINZ. *Theatergeschichte Europas.* (2nd ed.), Vol. I. Salzburg, 1966.
LÁZARO CARRETER, D. FERNANDO. *Teatro Medieval.* Valencia, 1958.
MANN, OTTO. *Geschichte des deutschen Dramas.* Stuttgart, 1963.
NICOLL, ALLARDYCE. *Masks, Mimes and Miracles.* New York, 1963.
PETIT DE JULLEVILLE, L. *Histoire du théâtre en France.* Paris, 1886.
RABY, F. J. E. *A History of Secular Latin Poetry.* Vol. II. Oxford, 1957.
RUDWIN, M. J. *The Origin of the German Carnival Comedy.* New York, 1920.
SHERGOLD, N. D. *A History of the Spanish Stage from Medieval Times Until the End of the Seventeenth Century.* Oxford, 1967.
WEEVERS, THEODOOR. *Poetry of the Netherlands in Its European Context 1170–1930.* Oxford, 1960.
YOUNG, KARL. *Drama of the Medieval Church.* 2 vols. Oxford, 1933.

The Play of Saint Nicholas
(LE JEU DE SAINT NICOLAS)

by Jean Bodel

"Officially" speaking, Jean Bodel's *Saint Nicholas* is a miracle play, that is to say a dramatic representation of a wonder wrought by the saint. It carries two distinctions simultaneously: it is the oldest (or shall we say youngest?) surviving French miracle play in the vernacular, and it is also the first genuine surviving French comedy. Perhaps we can call it a pseudo-didactic comedy. Written for a lay audience in town on the occasion of the saint's day, it could satisfy the conscience because of its ostentatious piety and then go on to its real job of tickling the secular rib. For in the year 1200 farce did not undermine faith, and faith did not prohibit farce.

The town in this instance was Arras, capital of the northern province of Artois which had passed to the French crown in 1180. Arras was a part of the great urban movement of Flanders which, along with a similar movement in Italy, marks the transition from an agrarian and feudal Europe to a Europe of cities and commerce. Although notable for commerce and industry, Arras was largely "a city of bankers," as Henri Pirenne describes it; that is to say, in the words of a contemporary poet, "full of riches, avid of lucre and glutted with usurers." That, probably, was why it also displayed considerable cultural accomplishments. Arras itself and the area around it produced finely crafted wares, it had an active musical life, and boasted of several literary societies in which the works of local writers (*trouvères*) could be heard. Later the town was to acquire fame for its manufacture of tapestries—behind one of which old Polonius met his death. Since the five earliest extant French comedies and farces all come from this single town, we may suppose that in Arras as much as anywhere in Europe, the full-blown secular comedy received a decisive impetus.

Here Jean Bodel was born in 1165. Little is known about him, but it is characteristic of the Arrasian artist that his name is clearly affixed to his works. Bodel was a *trouvère* who belonged to the most important literary society of Arras, the *Confrérie de la Sainte Chandelle*. This guild was charged with the care and administration of a miraculous candle that had appeared to two rival minstrels in 1105, when the pestilence was ravaging Arras. The drippings of this candle had the power to cure the sick. Gradually, because of its origin, the pious foundation had become a literary society like many others in France, where prosperous and art-loving citizens mingled with professional artists. These *puys* performed the same function then as do our concert halls and theatres now, although they had several other purposes as well, clubhouse conviviality being one of them. Once in a while a mystery or miracle was produced by and for the members and perhaps their guests. Perhaps—but this is only a guess—secular skits livened some of the banquets even then.

In the year 1200 occurred a solemn transfer of the sacred candle from cramped quarters in a chapel of the St. Nicholas hospital to a larger oratory in town. Professor Warne has suggested that this might have been the occasion for Bodel's play. In any event, historians agree that the play belongs to the years 1200 or 1201, and that it is unquestionably a product of the *Puy d'Arras*.

These were times of high crusading fervor in and around Arras. Troops were being raised for the Fourth Crusade. Bodel himself declared that he would have taken the cross had he not fallen a victim of leprosy. Scholars have not failed to see

Bodel's play as a reflection of his zeal. Considering the drubbing the Crusaders get, it may be wiser to speak of a high degree of *interest*. As for Bodel himself, he was admitted to a leper colony near Arras in 1202, and died there in 1210. A single manuscript of *Saint Nicholas*, copied by a scribe a century later, was discovered in 1779. Among other surviving works by Bodel, we have his *Farewell* to Arras, several fabliaux, and an epic about the Saxons.

Five known Saint Nicholas plays, all written in Latin, precede Bodel's work in twelfth-century France, attesting to the saint's popularity. Arras alone had two churches, three streets, and four houses named after him. The good bishop of Myra was also celebrated in song, narrative poetry, prose lives in both Latin and the vernacular, statuary, paintings, and stained glass. Bodel's work is therefore a further contribution rather than a pioneering enterprise. Like Greek tragedy, it gave the audience a fresh version of a cherished and familiar story. This story, however, should not rashly be called a legend. It is legend to us, but it was history, or at least quasi-history, to the twelfth- and thirteenth-century public. Unless we manage to feel the idea that this was heightened fact or poetic history to Bodel's audience, we must fail to understand the "cultural quality" of this and all other such plays in their own time.

Not only is Bodel's play the earliest surviving miracle in the vernacular, but, by general consent, it is also the best of them all. Its sophistication, astonishing when we consider its date, makes it unnecessary for us to adopt a patronizing tone or to tune our minds for a special historical reception. The story is essentially that of a Christian miracle operating in a heroic and a prosaic world, and proving its efficacy in both. But whereas in later masterpieces, such as *Pathelin* and *The Second Shepherds' Pageant*, the strands of the story are laid more or less side by side, here they are consummately intertwined. The epic events—the Christian invasion, the mustering of Saracens, the appearance of the Christian Knights, the battle and the slaughter—all serve to introduce the "Good

Christian," left alone on the battlefield and clutching his Saint Nicholas. Now if the testing of this "fetish" requires the previous epic events on one side, on the other it requires the thieves, who emerge therefore with the utmost naturalness out of their tavern in order to carry the action forward. When Saint Nicholas himself makes his unique appearance, it is to save the Christian, convert the infidel king, and rout the thieves. All three strands are braided into one piece.

At ease in his craft, Bodel handles his beginning, middle, and end without faltering. Every episode is logically linked to the next. Artful anticipations eliminate chance and accident. All motions are given their due time. Indeed, Bodel avoids abruptness and arbitrariness more efficiently than even Lope de Vega or Calderón did centuries later, not to speak of spurts and starts in the work of medieval dramatists. And if we cannot claim for him characterization in depth (which would be out of place in such a play to begin with), we admire how all the figures in the play assert themselves, from the choleric King (modeled on the Herod of Nativity plays and yet particularized) to the snarling jailer.

A detail which has been admired is our introduction to the first of the thieves, Clickett. Other playwrights of the Middle Ages summon their characters when they need them, but pay no attention to them before and after. Not so Bodel, who has the King's messenger stop for refreshment at an inn, where he runs into one of the ruffians who will later—much later— rob the Treasury. This done, Bodel introduces the second thief, drawn by the hawker's provocative description of the wines to be drunk on the premises. Still later the brains of the enterprise, Razor, walks in bringing news of the great opportunity in the Treasury. This is not a compact group like the three roisterers in Chaucer's *Pardoner's Tale* or like the dense groups in medieval painting and sculpture, but three lives marked off each from the other. At the end of the play, instead of simply dropping the thieves, Bodel tells us what their next prank will be, and again gives each one his particular destination.

When we come to the Christian warriors, we see only the

group, for one cannot individualize an army. But the Emirs, like the thieves, step forward each for himself, and one of them, the Emir of Arbisek, is memorable as the fierce and poor ruler who refuses to accept Christianity.[1] The universal literary practice was to convert or kill the Saracens on the last page. Bodel, inventive in so many places, decided to give his Emir all but the last word and thereby created a genuine and almost moving character.

From the point of view of ideology, what shall we think of this hero who refuses Christ? It is said that Bodel is always respectful of the Church, and yet the Emir's "I will not play the game" injects an equivocal note into the ideological purity of the play. The note is reinforced when we observe that the Christian hero is tearful and terrified, thinking only of his own safety instead of preaching to the infidels; that the executioner remains unimpressed even though the King is on his knees; and that the three thieves, though threatened with the gallows, are sent off by Bodel to pick other locks instead of joining in with the converts. These notes should not be overplayed, yet one is left wishing for a glimpse into Bodel's subconscious.

It was Chekhov who said that a pistol should not be introduced during the first act unless it is going to be discharged in the third. Bodel writes as if aware of this law of the well-made play. The early appearance of Clickett has already been mentioned. We are also forewarned that he will be leaving his clothes behind before the story is over. The reassurances of the Angel prepare us for the Good Christian's triumph. And most important, Tervagant's prophecy declares what is to follow, and is duly recalled at the end.

Order and coherence in the action; a keen feeling for the realities of tavern and town; love of the exotic and the fantastic; and a fresh sense of humor: these are the ingredients that make up Bodel's genius. Savoring these rowdies in the

[1] In the manuscript this refusal is ascribed to the Emir of Iconium. Speech ascriptions, however, are notably unreliable in this text, and I concur wholeheartedly with Albert Henry who gives the defiant speeches to the rude Arbisek.

tavern, the young waiter who promises to become another Snopes; the messenger who boasts he can outrace a camel; the King who snaps his teeth to reassure his Privy Councillor; an Emir who has marched on ice for thirty days to join the King; a Christian who almost faints when he sees the jailer's huge club, an idol that laughs, weeps, and drivels—relishing this and much more, we may well agree with Grace Frank when she observes that "if French drama had continued along similar lines, France need not have waited until 1830 for the 'romantic play.' "

Medieval writers, it is well known, paid little attention to historical accuracy. When we recollect that Clickett, Pinchdice, and Razor are "Saracens," we may wonder whether Bodel's audience was simply ignorant of differences between the Near East and their own Artois, or whether they recognized whimsy as well as we do, or as well as the audience, four hundred years later, that saw Bottom perform for King Theseus. I think it would be wise not to exaggerate the naïveté or plain stupidity of medieval burghers. They may have been fully aware that some of Bodel's geography was less than verifiable. And when one of the Saracen goons invokes Saint Nicholas before he rolls the dice—nothing is more common in medieval plays than these anachronistic or anatopistic oaths—we had better, all things considered, suppose that this rated a chuckle with the audience.

In the earlier Latin Saint Nicholas plays, the saint falls considerably short of spiritual greatness. He throws a tantrum because an infidel has insulted his image, or he is simply afraid of being further manhandled. When his triumph comes, it is reckoned by the cash he has preserved or multiplied. As P. R. Vincent has shown, Bodel's Saint Nicholas presents a substantial moral improvement. Bodel invented the personage of the Good Christian (or at any rate developed him from a mere hint or two in the older works), and thought of placing him in danger of death at the hands of the Saracens. He prays to the saint—his terror, as we have seen, is almost unseemly—and the saint intercedes to save his life. Thus Saint Nicholas is no longer the selfish and primitive godling jealous of his prerogatives, but a compassionate patron who helps his faithful servants when they are in need. It is not the loss of money that disturbs him, or the insult to his prestige, but the plight of a pious Christian. Still, he does restore stolen goods, and even multiplies them. Bodel did not neglect this part of the story, but he was clearly anxious to refine the flawed moral metal of the earlier saint.

Why the King exposes his treasures to robbery is another question. True, he is not much in love with Tervagant, but Bodel does not show him worrying after a new God. Perhaps, having just crushed the enemy, as Tervagant has predicted, he wonders whether the second half of the prediction, that he will adopt the Christian faith, will also come true. Unfortunately, Bodel does not mention this or any other motive in his text. Everywhere else, his motivation is impeccable. The King's challenge to Saint Nicholas must therefore be regarded as high fantasy and nothing more. Gratuitous gestures are the meat of storytellers everywhere. Explanations that call for motives, discover symbols, or dwell on "existential choices," are often guilty of dropping bombs on butterflies.

Saint Nicholas is a large play addressed to the ear and eye as well as the wit. The grotesque statue of Tervagant, the epic battle on stage, the colorful King and his Emirs, the Christian holding on to his "fetish," the frightful executioner with his club and his pincers, the dignified Angel (I like to think that music accompanied his speeches, as the violins sweetly mark Jesus' speeches in Bach's *St. Matthew Passion*), and the sudden appearance of Saint Nicholas himself—all these are grand visual effects that must have made Bodel's premiere a satisfying spectacle without injury to sense or order.

The staging makes use of the usual "mansions" of the medieval theatre. We see all the locations before us simultaneously: the palace, the Treasury, the jail, the tavern, something for the Faraway Lands, a place for the Angel, and a generalized space for street and battlefield. Once this is kept in mind, I do not think that the reader requires a profusion of stage directions.

For this version I have used Albert Henry's excellent edition of the play, published in Brussels in 1965. I have also made full use of the abundant material concerning Bodel's work in the technical journals.

The principle that has governed this "assimilation" of Bodel's text has been stated in the Introduction. The *lots* and *demi-lots* of wine are turned into the pitcher and half-pitcher to which we are accustomed. I have not made the smallest attempt to ascertain the comparative value between the *denier*, the *maille*, the *parti* of twelfth-century Arras and the American dollar and cent of 1970. I have simply used prices and amounts that will strike the reader of today as likely and natural, just as the prices and amounts named by Bodel seemed likely and natural to his spectators. For the dice games I acknowledge the gracious hand of my colleague J. Kent Clark, who must have spent his years in the Army more profitably than I, and who helped me update the original. Finally, I have made a few small and entirely inconsequential cuts.

BIBLIOGRAPHY

FRANK, GRACE. *The Medieval French Drama.* Oxford, 1960; first published in 1954. Chapter X concerns Bodel's play. Highly recommended.

VINCENT, P. R. *The Jeu de Saint Nicolas of Jean Bodel of Arras.* Baltimore, 1954. Particularly good on sources and background.

WARNE, F. J. (ed.). *Le Jeu de Saint Nicolas.* Oxford, 1958. This has an excellent introduction in English.

THE PLAY OF SAINT NICHOLAS

CHARACTERS

King of Africa and Arabia
King's Privy Councillor
Emir of Iconium
Emir of Hyrcania
Emir of Olifern
Emir of Arbisek
Oberon, the King's messenger
Tout, the King's herald
Duffy, jailer and executioner
Tervagant

Christian warriors
Angel
The Good Christian
Saint Nicholas

Innkeeper
Clip, a waiter
Rob, a town crier
Clickett, a thief
Pinchdice, another thief
Razor, another thief

In the palace.

OBERON: Great King, may your creator, our God Mahomet, save and protect you together with your lords! May he grant you the power to repel those who are attacking, ravaging, and wasting your land, the pestiferous Christians who neither worship nor honor our gods!
KING: What is this I hear? Apollo help me! Have the Christians

set foot in my empire? Are they foolhardy enough to make war against me?

OBERON: Sire, not since Noah built his ark has such a mighty army been seen. Even now their foragers are swarming over the land. The rogues and villains are putting our country to the torch. Oh King, if you do not act at once, your empire is ruined and destroyed.

KING (*To the statue of* TERVAGANT.): Tervagant, you son of a whore, is all this happening with your approval? Is it for this I covered your ugly face and body with gold? Let my oracle teach me this minute how to kill every last Christian, or else I swear I shall have you burned and melted down, and fling the gold that covers you to my rabble. (*To the* PRIVY COUNCILLOR.) I'm choking with anger. My rage is killing me.

COUNCILLOR: Your highness, these words are too rough! Not even a king is privileged to heap contempt on his gods. This is most reprehensible. But since my duty is to advise you, I say let us both prostrate ourselves before Tervagant with bare elbows and knees. Let us beg him to forgive us, so that we can smite the Christians through his holy power. Let us ask him to give us a trustworthy sign of his consent. Such is my loyal advice. Moreover, promise Tervagant another thick layer of gold to fatten his cheeks.

KING: I suppose you are right. Tervagant, my anger carried me away and made me talk like a fool. I should have kept my mouth shut, but I was as drunk as bread dunked in wine. Forgive me; you see I'm beating my breast and baring elbows and knees. Help me, oh Lord. Remember our holy law, which these Christians want us to forswear. They are even now spreading across my great kingdom. Teach us how to expel them. I am your friend. Reveal to me by a prophetic sign whether I shall be victorious. If I am to conquer, laugh. If I must be vanquished, cry. What is this? Tervagant laughed *and* cried! (*To the* PRIVY COUNCILLOR.) Interpret this for me! It must have a deep significance.

COUNCILLOR: This laughter, your highness, is undoubtedly a good omen. Well may you rejoice.

KING: Tell me the truth! By Mahomet, I command you as my Chief Councillor to expound this oracle to me.
COUNCILLOR: Although I owe you every obedience, sire, I had rather keep silent; I am afraid of your anger.
KING: Have no fear. I swear by all the gods that you're safe with me. Let it be like a game between us, a jest.
COUNCILLOR: My liege, I do trust you when you invoke all the gods. But I would feel even safer if you snapped your nail against your tooth.
KING: Here. This should satisfy you. It's the supreme oath. If you had murdered my own father I couldn't touch you now.
COUNCILLOR: Now my tongue is loosened, and the oracle shall be expounded at once. First Tervagant laughed. This means success for your arms. You shall vanquish the Christians on the same day you choose to attack them. But then Tervagant wept, and with good reason, for alas, alas, you are fated to deny and to renounce him. Thus it shall be.
KING: Five hundred curses light on the man who thinks so! If I hadn't snapped my nail against my tooth, Mahomet himself couldn't have saved you; I'd have torn you to pieces! Enough. Let's talk about something else. Go summon my warriors. Make them all come to the rescue, muster them from the Orient to Catalonia.
COUNCILLOR: Tout! Step forward! Make the proclamation!
TOUT (*In the street.*): Here ye, hear ye, all and sundry! Attend to my words, all who love their honor and their security! Let all armed men assemble about the King of Africa, the poor and the rich, from the land of Prester John to Iconium, soldiers of Alexandria, those of Cairo, the Kennelings, the Partichopes, and men of every warlike nation. Arm yourselves! Do not loiter! The punishment for disobedience is death! Do I hear you?[1]

---

[1] Here and later in the play, Tout concludes with what appears to have been a herald's formula: "That is all; now you can (should?) raise your clamor." According to Albert Henry, the herald is demanding a response from the citizenry. A director might tape a vociferous response and have it played at this point.

KING: Where is Oberon, my messenger?
OBERON: Here I am, your highness, at your command.
KING: Now, Oberon, let me see how nimble you are. Go summon the Giants and the Kennelings. Carry my letters every place, exhibit my royal seal, proclaim to all men that the Christians are spoiling my law. Warn those who hesitate that they and theirs will be slaves to the end of time. On your way! You should have been in the outskirts by now!
OBERON: Trust me, sire. I can leave a galloping camel behind.

(All leave.)

Enter the INNKEEPER *in front of his tavern.*

INNKEEPER: Welcome one and all! Best lunch in town served here! Welcome! Welcome! Good warm bread, fresh herring, the best wines by the barrel!

(Enter OBERON.*)*

OBERON: Thank God, another inn! (*To the* INNKEEPER.) What's to be had in your place?
INNKEEPER: Wine, my friend, thick enough to cut with a knife.
OBERON: Expensive?
INNKEEPER: Regular price, no extras, everything on the level. This is an honest establishment. Sit on the terrace, make yourself comfortable.
OBERON: I'll take a glass, my good man, but standing up. I'm not supposed to dawdle. Official business.
INNKEEPER: Whose?
OBERON: The King's. I'm carrying his message and his seal.
INNKEEPER: Try this. Guaranteed to go to your head. Down the hatch! The best part comes last.
OBERON: This glass has a false bottom. There was just enough to get my lips wet. Anyway, how much do I owe? I must be out of my mind staying this long.
INNKEEPER: You owe me seventy-five cents.

OBERON: All I've got is a dollar bill and a fifty-cent coin.
INNKEEPER: That's all right. I haven't got any change, so why don't you give me the dollar now, and on your way back I'll let you have a glass for fifty cents. As God is my witness, I should have charged you twice what I did. Give me the dollar, or else let me pour you a second glass.
OBERON: Why don't you take the fifty cents now and the dollar when I return?
INNKEEPER: Are you trying to kid me? You owe me seventy-five cents, my friend. And I'll have them before you leave the premises.
OBERON: But this is silly! I'm going to pay you a full dollar on my way back!
INNKEEPER: I get you. The year snow falls in June. It's no use, mister.
OBERON: Well, what am I supposed to do? Cut the fifty-cent piece in two?

(Enter CLICKETT.)

CLICKETT: Who's for killing time with a little game of dice? We'll play for small change.
INNKEEPER *(To OBERON.)*: You heard him. See if you can pay me out of his pocket.
OBERON: All right. Let's roll for a quarter.
CLICKETT: A quarter? Come on—we'll go for the six bits you owe.
OBERON: If it's all right with the boss.
CLICKETT *(To the INNKEEPER.)*: All right with you, ain't it?
INNKEEPER: Sure, provided nobody leaves the premises before I'm paid up.
OBERON *(To CLICKETT.)*: Roll 'em; one roll, high man wins, and don't load the dice.
CLICKETT: Here they go, they're clean. *(He rolls.)*
OBERON: Not bad. Two threes and a snake eye. Could be worse.
CLICKETT: A lousy seven! My usual bad luck.
OBERON: Be that as it may, it's my roll. Here goes. You count, my friend. Three fours in a row. Too bad!

CLICKETT: God damn these messengers! Slippery bastards!
OBERON: Landlord, this gentleman will settle for me. He has insulted me, but I've got a thick skin.
INNKEEPER: On your way! *(To* CLICKETT.*)* You bit off more than you could chew.

(All leave.)

Faraway lands. OBERON *reappears.*

OBERON: May Mahomet protect the Emir of Iconium, whom the King is summoning to his aid!
EMIR OF ICONIUM: Oberon, instruct the King on my behalf that I intend to join him with a mighty host. Tell him that nothing on earth will hold me back.

*(*OBERON *moves on.)*

OBERON: May Mahomet protect and bless you, mighty Emir of Hyrcania! I have been sent by the King to require your help.
EMIR OF HYRCANIA: Mahomet save your soul, Oberon. Go on your way. Since the King demands it, I shall depart this very day.

*(*OBERON *moves on.)*

OBERON: May our God Mahomet, who reigns over all things, protect you, great Emir of Olifern. The King has sent me to summon you.
EMIR OF OLIFERN: Oberon, assure the King that I will support him with all my forces, and that I would not fail him for the world.

*(*OBERON *moves on.)*

OBERON: Emir of Arbisek, the King of Africa and Arabia commands you to succor him without delay, for the Christians are waging war against him.
EMIR OF ARBISEK: Oberon, tomorrow at dawn I shall leave at the head of a hundred thousand heathens.

All leave. OBERON *returns to the palace.*

OBERON: Your Majesty, may Mahomet save and protect you and yours.
KING: And may he bless you, Oberon. Do you bring good news?
OBERON: Your Highness, I have done so well, scouting through Arabia and every heathen land, that there never was a king who assembled even a tenth of the crowd of pagan counts, kings, princes, and barons that I have mustered for you.
KING: Go take a rest, friend Oberon.

(Exit OBERON; *enter the* EMIR OF ICONIUM.*)*

EMIR OF ICONIUM: I salute you, sire, in the name of Apollo and Mahomet. Behold, I am here to serve you as becomes a faithful vassal.
KING: Wisely done, my dear friend. Always come when I call you.
EMIR OF ICONIUM: Your Majesty, I have sped from the land where the grickles grow, far beyond the Neronian field, because of the dangers which beset you. I have walked thirty days on ice with hobnailed boots. I believe I deserve your love.

(Enter the EMIR OF HYRCANIA.*)*

KING: What is this army?
EMIR OF HYRCANIA: Sire, these men are from beyond the Gray Wallings, where the very turds of dogs are made of gold. Will you bestow your love on me? I have ordered a hundred vessels filled with my treasures to sail into your harbor.
KING: My good Emir, I am heartily sorry for all the trouble you are taking.

(Enter the EMIR OF OLIFERN.*)*

KING: And where do you come from?
EMIR OF OLIFERN: From beyond Mecca, sire, a vast and hot domain. I am not niggardly with you, oh King, for I have brought you thirty chariots full of rubies and emeralds.

(Enter the EMIR OF ARBISEK.)

KING: And you, the man who is staring at me, where do you come from?
EMIR OF ARBISEK: From beyond Arbisek. I can bring you nothing, sire, for in my land millstones are our only coin.
KING: Well, here's a fine gift of poverty for me!
EMIR OF ARBISEK: Your Majesty, in our land—and this is the truth—one man can carry a hundred of these coins in his purse.
COUNCILLOR: My liege, since these lords have all answered your summons, order them to attack the Christians at once.
KING: I will, by Mahomet! I'll give these Christians a bellyfull of war. Every mother's son of them must be killed, caught, or driven out. Go tell these lords in my name to take the best possible measures.
COUNCILLOR: My lords, I bid you all in the King's name to confound the Christian religion. Your duty, gentlemen, is to slaughter the enemy. He must be repaid for the ills he has made us suffer. Go at once. The King wills it.
ALL THE EMIRS TOGETHER: Let us go, and may Mahomet help us!

They leave. The CHRISTIAN WARRIORS *appear on the battlefield.*

A CHRISTIAN: Forward, by Saint Sepulcher!
ANOTHER: My lords, on to noble deeds!
ANOTHER: The pagans and the Saracens are coming to crush us!
ANOTHER: See how these weapons shine! I'm the happiest man on earth!
ANOTHER: Stun them with our valor!
ANOTHER: They're a hundred to one, my lords!
ONE OF THE CHRISTIANS: My lords, let there be no mistake, this is the last day of our lives. We shall all die doing God's work on earth. But as long as my sword is whole, I intend to sell my life at a high rate and to hack through many a Saracen

armor. My lords, we must be ready to lay down our lives in the service of God. It will be paradise for us, and hell for them. See to it, my friends, that they taste our iron.

A NEWLY KNIGHTED CHRISTIAN: I am young, my lords, but don't belittle me! A young body often holds a mighty heart. There is a heathen warrior in the distance, the strongest of them all—I have been watching him, and unless he kills me first I mean to strike him dead.

AN ANGEL:[2] Lords, be of good cheer. I am a messenger of God. He will soon put an end to your troubles. Trust him. The unbelievers are ready to fling themselves upon you, but do not falter, offer your lives boldly to God, and take here the death of the faithful whose hearts are with the Lord.

A CHRISTIAN: Who are you, bright creature, bringing us words of encouragement and high meaning from God? Though you speak the truth, know that we shall face our mortal enemy with undaunted hearts.

ANGEL: I am an angel sent by God, dear friend, to comfort you. Take heart, for he shall seat you with the elect in heaven. Continue as you have begun. You must be slaughtered, all of you, but a glorious crown awaits you hereafter. Now I must be gone. You, remain with God.

(Exit the ANGEL. *The heathens appear.)*

EMIR OF ICONIUM: Lords, as the oldest among you, I have already given you a great deal of excellent advice. We are all experienced fighters. Let us not allow any Christian we meet to escape.

EMIR OF HYRCANIA: Escape? These sons of whores? Watch me strike and see whether I leave a single Christian standing up.

EMIR OF ICONIUM: I too, on my side, intend to cut them down like a reaper in a cornfield.

EMIR OF OLIFERN: My fine cutthroats, aren't you going to leave a couple of Christians to me?

---

[2] T. B. W. Reid suggests that the Angel speaks throughout the play from a rostrum or a pulpit in his own distinct place.

EMIR OF ARBISEK: Here comes the hated race! Soldiers of Mahomet, forward! Strike, strike, all together!

(Now the Saracens kill all the CHRISTIANS.)[3]

EMIR OF HYRCANIA: My lords, hurry over here! The marvels we have seen are nothing compared to this prisoner of mine! Take a look at this grizzled villain who is clutching his fetish.[4] Shall we kill him or take him alive?

EMIR OF OLIFERN: Let's not kill him. We'll show him off to the King as an oddity. Get up, you rascal, and come along.

EMIR OF ARBISEK: Hold him, men. I'll take care of his fetish.

GOOD CHRISTIAN: Help, Saint Nicholas! Protect me from these tormentors!

(All leave.)

ANGEL: Knights who lie here, how fortunate you are! How justly you now despise the world in which you suffered! And in exchange for your woes, you know, do you not, how precious is the paradise in which God places those he loves. Let all men imitate your death, for God receives into his gentle bosom whoever desires to come to him. As for you, good Christian, though you were led away by traitors, fear nothing, place your trust in God, and after God in Saint

---

[3] This stage direction is in the manuscript. We must imagine an extremely lively and reasonably lengthy fight at this point, not without ad libs and Shakespearean drums, trumpets, and alarums.

[4] This grizzled villain, who will presently speak, is called "Li Preudom" in the original, that is to say the wise, good, reliable, respected man—the perfect elderly gentleman, in short. What is he doing amidst these warriors on a battlefield in heathendom? He is not a reporter or a cook, after all. Oddly enough, scholars have unanimously overlooked this small yet singular problem. Here is a guess: Bodel would have liked to make his Preudom a priest or a monk accompanying the Christian army, but thought—or was advised—that such a figure would be indecorous for the comic stage, either in general or in the particular circumstance for which his play was written. Be that as it may, the Gentleman might well become a priest or monk in a modern production. The fetish that he clutches is called "horned" in the original—a reference to St. Nicholas' miter; but I have dropped the adjective.

Nicholas, who will comfort you in your need when he sees your faith unshaken.[5]

In the palace.

EMIR OF ICONIUM: King of Africa and Arabia, happier than happy! Through our valor, through our wisdom, your war is concluded. The miserable invaders are dead. Their bodies litter the countryside four leagues in every direction.

KING: Well done, my lords. But tell me, who is that sorry-looking hooded rogue you have brought along? He's the ugliest villain I have ever seen.

EMIR OF ICONIUM:[6] Your Majesty, we kept him alive in order to entertain you with a marvel. We discovered him on his knees, hands clasped, weeping and praying to some kind of wooden puppet he adores.

KING: Come closer. Tell me, wretch, do you really believe in this image?

GOOD CHRISTIAN: I do, your highness, by the holy cross! And so should the entire world.

KING: Tell me why, you dog.

GOOD CHRISTIAN: This is Saint Nicholas. He helps those who are in need. He finds that which is lost. He shows wayfarers the path from which they strayed. He leads unbelievers to the true faith. He restores their vision to the blind. He revives those who have drowned. Nothing he guards can vanish or deteriorate, no matter how forsaken, how neglected. Were this palace filled with gold, it would be

---

[5] In the original, the Emirs and their prisoner are still on stage when the Angel speaks. I have removed them for the sake of plausibility. When the Angel addresses the Good Christian, the little group might reappear "in the distance," on their way to the palace. In this way the heathens can be shown unaware of the Angel's presence, while the Christian receives the message of comfort in his soul.

[6] This speech is assigned to the Privy Councillor in the manuscript, one of many similar slips made by the copyist. This one has not been caught by previous editors.

safe while my Saint Nicholas rested upon it. Such is the power that God has infused in him.

KING: We'll soon discover how true this is, you rogue. We'll test your Saint Nicholas. I'll entrust my treasure to him, and if I miss so much as the weight of a splinter in my eye, I'll have you burned alive or broken on the wheel. My lord, hand him over to Duffy, our chief torturer, and don't let him get away.

(The PRIVY COUNCILLOR *leads the* GOOD CHRISTIAN *to jail.)*

COUNCILLOR: Duffy, Duffy, open the jail!
DUFFY: Come in, and don't mind if I don't welcome you.
GOOD CHRISTIAN: What a huge club you're carrying, sir.
DUFFY: Step down into this dungeon; it was pining away for you. Guess I'll be keeping my pincers busy while you're in my clutches and there's a tooth left in your ugly mouth.

(The GOOD CHRISTIAN *enters his cell. The* ANGEL *appears to him.)*

ANGEL: Good Christian, lift up your heart and have no fear. Trust the true Savior and trust Saint Nicholas, for I know he will come to your help. You shall convert the King and tear his lords away from their mad religion and lead them to the Christian faith.
GOOD CHRISTIAN: With all my heart I believe in Saint Nicholas.

(Exit.)

In the palace.

COUNCILLOR: He is in jail, your Majesty.
KING: Well now, my good friend, I want all my treasures, everything I own, coffers and drawers, spread open, and Saint Nicholas placed on top.

(The PRIVY COUNCILLOR *proceeds as told.)*

COUNCILLOR: Your command is executed, sire. The soldiers and guards have been dismissed. Now you can go to sleep.

KING: Good. But if I lose so much as a penny, let the villain tremble! Amazing how he trusts his god! Now let my herald proclaim this matter to the whole population.
COUNCILLOR: Tout, come here! Proclaim throughout the kingdom that the King's treasure has been left unattended. It's a lucky day for thieves!
TOUT *(In the street.)*: Hear ye, hear ye! Gather round and attend to my words. In the King's name I let it be known that the locks and chains have been struck off his treasures. I say his treasures are yours as if they were lying before you on the ground. Let anyone who is able carry everything away, for there is only one guard left, a fetish, stone dead, for it never stirs. That is all. Do I hear you? *(Uproar.)*

Outside the tavern. The INNKEEPER *and* CLIP *appear.*

INNKEEPER: Business is bad, Clip my boy. Call Rob and tell him to hawk my wine for awhile. It's beginning to look as if people were tired of drinking.
CLIP: Hey Rob, the boss wants you to bring in some customers. Hustle a bit, will you?

(Enter TOUT.*)*

TOUT: I heard that. What do you think you're doing? Trying to muscle me out of my job? Stepping on my toes? I advise you to keep your mouth shut.
ROB: Who are you to tell me what to do?
TOUT: My name is Tout, official herald in this city by right of birth; a job I've made my living at these sixty years. And who are you?
ROB: My name is Rob. I'm an independent.[7]
TOUT: Get out of my sight, you pipsqueak! You're not worth the hole in my sock.

---

[7] In the original, Tout derives his privilege from the aldermen, and Rob from the "hommes de la ville," another branch of the Arras administration. This was a recent division, and Bodel is amusing his audience here with a scene of local politics.

ROB: Are you shoving me around?

TOUT: That's what it looks like, and thank your stars I ain't layin' you out flat on the cobblestones. Don't interfere with my job, that's all.

ROB: Look who's trying to push me around! I'm warning you, don't talk too big or you might get yourself clobbered before you know it.

CLIP: Boss, Rob and Tout are fighting in the street—professional rivalry!

INNKEEPER: Stop it, gentlemen, easy does it! Down, Rob, easy, Tout. Tell me what the trouble is, I'll be the umpire.

ROB: All right with me.

TOUT: With me too. Go ahead and settle this.

INNKEEPER: Leave it to me. Each of you is going to stick to his own territory. Tout, you've got the official proclamations for the King and the city council. And Rob can make a living spreading the good word about our excellent wines. For all I care, he can be drunk on the job as long as he's doing it. That's all. Kiss and make up. I don't want any quarrels on my doorstep.

ROB: All right, Tout, let's make peace.

TOUT: Peace it is. Go hustle as much as you like. *(Exit.)*

ROB: Come taste, come taste our wine! A freshly-opened barrel of wine that's savory, supple, solid, and succulent, rising up like a squirrel in the woods, leaving not a trace of mold or sour, thickened in its lees, full-bodied, firm, nervy, as limpid as a sinner's tears, and lingering long on the tongues of connoisseurs—all others kindly stay away!

(Enter PINCHDICE.)

PINCHDICE: Let's have a taste, friend; I'm a connoisseur if there ever was one.

ROB *(Pouring.)*: Look at it foam! Look at it leap and sizzle and glitter! Don't gulp it down. Roll it over your tongue a bit. This is no ordinary wine, it's an ultra-wine.

PINCHDICE: Not bad, not bad at all! Brings me back to life.

THE PLAY OF SAINT NICHOLAS

CLICKETT *(From the tavern.)*: Look who's here! Pinchdice! Welcome, old pal, I've missed you! Come on in!

PINCHDICE: Jesus, when I think of the times we've been drunk together!

CLICKETT: How about a drink right now? I've already imbibed —and hocked my clothes, too.

PINCHDICE: As long as there's some left in the cellar, I'm available.

(They enter the tavern.)

CLICKETT: Clip, bring us half a pitcher.

CLIP *(To the* INNKEEPER.*)*: You might be wise to settle with Mr. Clickett before he starts chalking up more drinks.

INNKEEPER: Mr. Clickett, you already owe me for a full pitcher—that's three dollars. Then for last week's game, one dollar. And the seventy-five cents you lost today. Altogether pretty close to five dollars.

CLICKETT: Make it an even five. I don't care. I never argue with the owner.

INNKEEPER: Right. Clip, the best for Mr. Pinchdice, of course.

CLIP: Is this how you'll get rich? *(He serves the wine.)*

CLICKETT: Damn you, Clip, do you call this a half pitcher? Here's a fellow that goes regular to church every Sunday and robs his customers blind on weekdays.

PINCHDICE: Give us a candle at least and do something useful for a change.

CLIP: Here's a candle. That's two dollars, including the wine.

CLICKETT: You're no slouch when it comes to adding up, that's a fact.

PINCHDICE: Pour, Clickett, I need it bad, my lips are cracking with the thirst.

CLICKETT: All you like. Who's stopping you? Drink up and God help you.

PINCHDICE: God, this is all right. Ice cold. Drink, old pal. This is first-rate stuff. The owner don't know what he's selling. It's worth five bucks a pitcher.

CLICKETT: Pipe down; he'll overhear you; or else his pickpocket of a waiter will.
PINCHDICE: Clip here? Who bleeds the barrel when the boss ain't lookin' and forgets to pay for it?
CLIP: Gentlemen, not another word on this subject, do you mind?
CLICKETT: We're just kidding, Clip. Come on, let's drink in peace and harmony. There's a drop left here and the candle's still burning.

(Enter RAZOR.)

RAZOR: God save you, gentlemen of the guard! I am a happy man. Here are my own Clickett and Pinchdice whom I've been aching to see.
CLICKETT: Sit down, Razor, and take a dip with us.
RAZOR: Gentlemen, my reply is an unhesitating yes. Aren't we three hearts beating as one?
PINCHDICE: Fill his glass, Clickett.
CLICKETT: Liquid velvet in your gullet. You're in luck today, Razor. *(RAZOR drinks.)* Look at him! He's caught up with us already!
RAZOR: This is nothing, gentlemen. If you'd emptied ten pitchers, I'd still share the expense with you. We're friends, aren't we? Clip, come here; fetch us a full decanter. God willing, I'll even pay you.
CLICKETT: Razor must have struck gold. He's giving orders like a banker.
RAZOR: Trust me, friends, and keep lapping it up—everything will be taken care of. Money means nothing to me. If our host is willing to wait till daybreak tomorrow, he'll be royally paid.
PINCHDICE: Listen to the man! He must have dreamed he dug up a treasure.
RAZOR: Come on, don't be chicken, drink like men!
CLICKETT: Razor my buddy, we've downed so much wine we'll have to pawn our duds for it.
CLIP: Here you are, Mr. Clickett. That's another five dollars; three for this pitcher, and two for the half you had before.

THE PLAY OF SAINT NICHOLAS 59

PINCHDICE: Is this stuff pure?
CLIP: Sure it is; I'll swear it on the cross.
RAZOR: Pour, Clickett, pour, don't be shy; we'll finish this and then we'll see if there's more in the cellar. Nobody worry about the score.
PINCHDICE: You been eating herring or something? Look at him slurping it up!
CLICKETT: Never mind. He's on to something. I can tell.
RAZOR: Whatever it is, down the pipe and farewell grief! Pour like it was plain beer, Clickett old friend.
PINCHDICE: Come on, we're all paying for the entertainment, but you ain't cuttin' us in on your bankroll. You're awful cocky today. What happened last night? Did you crack a safe maybe?
RAZOR: I did no such thing. But I'm counting on certain favorable news that's come my way.
PINCHDICE: You'll let us in on it, I hope.
RAZOR: Come on boys, more drinking and less talking. We're about to recoup all our expenditures. The warehouses of the Lord are open. Nothing stands in the way of our making a killing. The King of Africa has thrown locks, chains, and bolts out the window, his guards have gone home, all the treasures are ours for the taking. They've stretched a fetish out on top of the heap, wood or stone, I don't know which, all I know is that it won't open its mouth to tell the King who came and hauled off the loot. Today's our day, fellows. When the right moment comes, the three of us are going in.
PINCHDICE: Is this all true?
RAZOR: Positively. I heard the proclamation myself. The treasures are out in the open, the guards are gone, everybody is free to help himself if he's able. Fair enough, I say.
CLICKETT: Pour him another glass, Pinchdice. The man has spoken words of gold.
PINCHDICE: Here you are, old pal, and what's more, I want you to hear my solemn promise. Next time I play, I swear that my first winnings are yours, no matter where or when. No fooling, see?

CLICKETT: Say, how about a game right now?

PINCHDICE: Right! Loser to pay out of the loot we're gonna rake in if we're lucky.

CLICKETT *(To the* INNKEEPER.*)*: Listen, brother, I want you to lend me a tenner. That'll be sixteen altogether I owe you, including interest.

INNKEEPER: Mr. Clickett, remember you're borrowing money.[8] I'm sure you realize that I'm entitled to solid security. You've got a nice overcoat, it fits you perfectly, but I'm afraid it's going to remain behind when you leave this inn tonight.

PINCHDICE: Relax, man, relax. You don't know which way the wind is blowing. Well, men, we've drunk up five dollars' worth tonight. Let's roll for those first.

CLICKETT: Who's got dice?

PINCHDICE: Me. Latest style. Perfect cubes. Each one the same size and weight.

RAZOR: Put them back in your pocket, my friend. *(To* CLICKETT.*)* I hope you don't mind.[9]

CLICKETT: Why should I? Where's Clip? Come here, Clip, and lend us your dice, will you? You'll get a cut out of the stake. Besides, we're on to something big—whatever it is, you won't be sorry if you play ball with us.

CLIP: I'm willing to cooperate, Mr. Clickett. *(He goes for the dice.)*

PINCHDICE: What's it gonna be, you two? Do we split the tab or do we play for it?

---

[8] From these words we can assume, I think, that the Innkeeper is handing the money over. I have omitted a few inexplicable lines in which the Innkeeper tells Clickett that the latter is adding up wrong. But as he tallies Clickett's debts, they come out to what we already know and Clickett admitted to, namely five dollars. The passage in question would have made sense only if the Innkeeper had charged Clickett with the *new* five dollars that Pinchdice and Razor have run up, but this he does not do.

[9] Implying that Clickett and Pinchdice might well be accomplices. It will be remembered that Razor came in last and found the other two together.

THE PLAY OF SAINT NICHOLAS

RAZOR: Let's roll for it, men. The loser picks up the check.
CLICKETT: Clip, damn you, where's them dice?
CLIP: Here they are, here they are. Handle them carefully, will you? They're on the level—I've had them registered at City Hall.
RAZOR: All right, men. Let's play for all we're going to drink till tomorrow morning.
PINCHDICE: Everybody shoot with hands wide open.
RAZOR: Right.
CLICKETT: Sure thing.
PINCHDICE: You first, Razor, and no tricks.

(RAZOR *tosses.*)

RAZOR: Three fives!
PINCHDICE: Sweet Lord in heaven, give me all sixes. *(He throws.)*
CLICKETT: Ha ha ha! Not by a mile, my boy. You're gonna be leaving your shirt with the pawnbroker's. Anyway, you got a total of five for five dollars, it's a good rule to follow, and we all know you can count that high.
PINCHDICE: Damn you and don't bother to shoot.
RAZOR: That's right, you don't want to humiliate him.
CLICKETT *(To* PINCHDICE.*)*: Okay, you pick up the bill; everything's fair and square.
PINCHDICE: How about a game for straight cash?
CLICKETT: I'm willing.
RAZOR: Me too. Open your purses, men. Everybody place three singles on the table. If you haven't got the cash, get a loan. Winner take all. No cheating possible.
CLICKETT: How do we play?
PINCHDICE: Anything you want.
CLICKETT: High man takes all?
PINCHDICE: Fine with me.
RAZOR: I'll go first. Dear God, be good to me.
CLIP: Hold it a minute. How can anybody see in the dark? Here's another candle.
PINCHDICE: That's my boy. Treat us square and you won't be sorry when the time comes.

(RAZOR *rolls.*)

RAZOR: Twelve! Thank you, Lord.

PINCHDICE: Four, four, and deuce. Excuse me, but in my books that adds up to ten.

RAZOR: Which God willing will be more than you'll ever see. Go on, you'll be lucky if you throw a nine.

PINCHDICE: Oh yeah? The hell with you. I'll be damned if I can't top your lousy ten.

CLIP: Meantime who's paying for the candle? (*He picks up one of the dollars.*) Here's my due, anyway. Waiting on people like you is enough to drive a man to the nuthouse.

CLICKETT: Hey, hey, put down our dough. Wait till we're finished.

CLIP: I won't. Look, you're using up our candles, and all the help has to hang around until you're finished playing.

PINCHDICE: The boy is right. Let's hurry up. My turn. (*He rolls.*) Not interested, Razor old friend?

RAZOR: No, because you're one point ahead of me.

CLICKETT: My turn now. I can throw an eleven with two dice, and the third brings in the pot. (*He rolls.*)

PINCHDICE: No good! Roll again! Your sleeve was over your hand!

CLICKETT: Keep talking while I pocket what's coming to me. Two fours and a six, see?

PINCHDICE: Put that money down before it's too late! And I don't mean tomorrow!

CLICKETT: What's biting you? Do I or don't I win by three points?

PINCHDICE: I'm telling you to lay the money on the table before I get mad.

CLICKETT: I'll see you damned in hell first. The dice don't lie.

PINCHDICE: That roll didn't count! Can you hear me? And you ain't gonna force it to count!

CLICKETT: Let go of me! You're tearing my coat off!

PINCHDICE (*Hitting him.*): Here's one for you. You're no match for me, kid.

CLICKETT: Think you're scaring me? Take that.

CLIP: Boss, boss! Here goes our security! They're ripping each other's clothes! And God knows they weren't worth much to begin with!

INNKEEPER: Fighting in my place? Clickett, Pinchdice, sit down, both of you, let's settle this without bloodshed. What happened, Mr. Razor? Tell me—you should know.

RAZOR: Ask Clip who's at fault. All I want is peace.

CLICKETT: All right, Clip, you be the judge.

PINCHDICE: Go ahead.

CLIP: Well then, start off by putting the money on the table—all of it.

CLICKETT: Here's the eight bucks. Go on now, decide, and let's keep it in the family.

CLIP: Gentlemen, you've made me the arbiter of this dispute. As such, I require two of these bills for myself. The other six are to be shared equally among the three of you, because if one of you took them all there would be more fireworks. Mr. Clickett, pour wine into the glasses, give Mr. Pinchdice a drink, and be friends again. That's my decision.

CLICKETT: Okay, Pinchdice, I apologize. And as a token of peaceful intentions, I'm pouring your wine.

PINCHDICE: I forgive you, Clickett. I know you did it under the influence.

CLICKETT: Let's go on to something else, men, so that we can all pay our debts to our host. The night's far gone already; the moon is down; and we're not making any money here.

RAZOR (*To the* INNKEEPER.): Come on, my friend, let's see you make a gesture of good will. True, we owe you a little money, but we know where to go for it. I assure you that the take will be tremendous. We are going to dip freely into a great treasure, and we'll come back to you groaning under the weight of gold and silver. I am offering you a deal the likes of which you have never dreamed of. Here, in this very saloon, you will oversee the distribution of the loot; you will draw lots for us; and one part of the booty will be yours. With a guarantee of this magnitude, I trust you'll be willing to extend credit to us without a shadow of fear.

INNKEEPER: Can I really trust the guy?
CLICKETT: One hundred percent. If we don't get caught and don't take a trip to the gallows, you'll wind up with a tank full of fine gold. Matter of fact, why don't you lend us a large sack to put the stuff in?
INNKEEPER: Go get a sack, Clip. God willing, I'll get paid.
CLIP: Here's one that'll hold two bushels. Hope you come back all in one piece.
PINCHDICE: So long, friend, and keep your fingers crossed for us.
INNKEEPER: I will, gentlemen. God be with you.

In the street.

RAZOR: Pinchdice, you're the expert. Go find out if the King's asleep, and don't make any noise.

(PINCHDICE goes and comes back.)

PINCHDICE: All right, guys, make it quick, the King and his bigwigs are sleeping like they were dead.

(They go into the Treasury.)

RAZOR: He must be tired of being rich, putting this doll in charge of his treasure.
CLICKETT: Here, take this casket, it's full of doubloons.
RAZOR: Holy devil, is it heavy! Pinchdice, bring the sack closer. This box weighs a ton. It's killing me.
PINCHDICE: Shove it in, all of it, I ain't gonna leave nothing behind. I don't care if I poop out. Lemme try my strength, I'll show you who can do it. Help me load if you can. *(They help him load the sack on his shoulder.)*
CLICKETT: That does it. Let's get out of here while the coast is clear.

(They return to the tavern.)

RAZOR: Landlord! Open up! We've come back with a bulging sack! Honest to God!

THE PLAY OF SAINT NICHOLAS 65

INNKEEPER: Welcome, welcome! Clip, give the men a hand, hurry up! So glad to see you back! *(They enter the tavern.)*
PINCHDICE: I've worked like a horse. Gimme a drink, somebody. I deserve one.
CLICKETT: That he does. A stiff drink'll fix him up again.
INNKEEPER: Gentlemen, there's a fire waiting for you, upholstered chairs, and booze fit for monarchs.
RAZOR *(To* CLIP.*)*: Go open the spigot, friend, and give it to us foaming.
CLICKETT: And make him get us a couple of candles, will you?
INNKEEPER: You heard the orders, Clip.
CLIP: Here's the candles, and the best wine in the house.
RAZOR: Blessed be the hour in which this wine was put in the cask!
CLICKETT *(Drinking.)*: Oh God, if this don't hit the spot! For once there's no shortage.
PINCHDICE: Keep the pitcher circulating; I've got another date with it.
CLICKETT: Go on, drink all you want, but don't swallow the glass!
PINCHDICE: I can't seem to get rid of my thirst.
CLIP: Do you want my dice again?
RAZOR: Excellent suggestion.
PINCHDICE: Time for a good game.
CLICKETT: Plenty in the pot, too.
RAZOR: All of it on loan from the gallows.
PINCHDICE: Ready, everybody? Let's shoot crap this time. I'm in the chips tonight.
RAZOR: Everybody get down his bet, and may the best man win.
CLICKETT: I'm going down the mine shaft. *(He digs into the sack.)* Is this good enough?
PINCHDICE: Here's my share. Should be worth as much as yours.
RAZOR: My part's about the same, too.
INNKEEPER: Is it my turn now, gentlemen? Shall we settle? It should be easy.
CLICKETT: When the time comes to divvy up, you'll get your share, don't worry.

PINCHDICE: Okay, let's see who gets to roll. High man handles the dice. Nobody touch that table.
RAZOR: Don't wobble it. It's as level as a table can be.
CLICKETT: I don't think so. It's higher on your side.
PINCHDICE: You're wrong, Clickett. Bet you a gold nugget you're wrong.
RAZOR: You can place a pea in the middle. If anything, it'll roll toward me.
CLICKETT: Forget it and shoot.[10]
PINCHDICE: Off they go! *(RAZOR rolls.)* Let's see what you got.
CLICKETT: Looks like a grubby four.
RAZOR: These dice are slippery!
PINCHDICE: Come on, Razor, it's your hand that was sweating. Look at me. I rub my palm in the dust, and then—away they go. Box cars! Let's see you beat that.
CLICKETT: No use my trying. He's got the dice, Razor. All right, guys. Gold on the table.
RAZOR *(Aside to CLICKETT.)*: Keep your eye on his hand.
CLIP: You'll need more light, gentlemen. Here, Mr. Clickett, take this extra candle.
CLICKETT: After the dice have spoken, Clip, you'll get a dollar from each of us.
CLIP: Why not right now, before you start?
PINCHDICE: Lay off, pal, you're putting us to sleep always singing the same tune.
INNKEEPER: Leave them alone, Clip. They're going to treat us right.
RAZOR: We will, my good man. You can think of me as if I were your other self.
INNKEEPER: God bless you.
PINCHDICE: I'm ready, fellows. And I'm playing for the whole pot.
CLICKETT: Come on snake eyes!
PINCHDICE: Seven or eleven, by God, come on seven! *(He rolls.)*
RAZOR: Nine! Now let's see a seven.

[10] They are using two dice now.

PINCHDICE: Never! *(To* CLICKETT.*)* Quit breathing down my neck, will you? You don't give me room enough to shake the dice.

CLICKETT: All right, roll 'em, hands open, and make it a seven by all the rotten luck I've had!

(PINCHDICE rolls again.)

PINCHDICE: Eight! Well, it beats a seven anyway.

CLICKETT: Damn those fidgety fingers of yours!

(PINCHDICE rolls again.)

PINCHDICE: Five! Not bad.

CLICKETT: Seven, baby, seven!

PINCHDICE: Come on, you nine, wind up the game.

CLICKETT: Nine minus two, Saint Nicholas!

(PINCHDICE rolls again.)

PINCHDICE: A friendly nine! *(He gathers up the stakes.)* Come to daddy, little children. Here's my happy family!

RAZOR: Now that's done, Pinchdice, hand it over to me. Remember your promise. You swore you'd give me your first winnings as a present. This is it.

PINCHDICE: You're outa your mind, damn you to hell! This is *wealth* we're talking about! You think I'm some kind of nincompoop? I made that promise when we was putting up petty cash. Sure, next time we play for a drink or two I'll—

RAZOR: Keep yapping, Pinchdice, but a promise is a promise.

PINCHDICE: Ain't you ashamed to spoil our luck?

RAZOR: Everything that's on the table is mine, my boy.

PINCHDICE: Yeah? You'll have to carry me along with it.

RAZOR: Let go!

PINCHDICE: Hands off, or I'll slash your eyes!

CLIP: Boss, they're at it again! They're murdering one another!

INNKEEPER: What's going on? Are you crazy, Pinchdice? Let him go. You too, Mr. Razor. Sit down, both of you. I know what the source of the trouble is. Leave it all to me; I'll see that both of you get satisfaction.

PINCHDICE *(Surrendering the money.)*: All right, here's the dough.
RAZOR *(The same.)*: This is against my better judgment.
INNKEEPER: Mr. Clickett, take all these coins and put them back in that box.
CLICKETT: Good idea. I've got them all, I think.
INNKEEPER: This way we're all equal, like when we started. Everything is common. And now let's each of us four take his rightful share. Well, what are you waiting for?
RAZOR: I'll tell you what. We're all bushed. Don't forget we've been up most of the night. We'll share and share alike, but first we'd better get some sleep.

(All leave.)

In the palace.

COUNCILLOR: Alas! Apollo and Mahomet stand by me! I have had a nightmare about the King's treasure. It seemed to me that the earth had collapsed under it and that it was sinking forever into the abyss of hell. I won't be easy until I have seen it again. *(He inspects the Treasury.)* Your Majesty! A catastrophe! Awake, rise, unhappy King! God strike the man who won't help you now! Your treasure has been carried off!
KING: What's the matter? Who's waking me up? What are you saying?
COUNCILLOR: My liege, you are a penniless beggar. But don't blame anyone except yourself. The greatest treasure that ever was—you entrusted it to a man of wood. Here he lies on the floor. Look at him.
KING: Is it true? Have I lost all my wealth? That hoary rascal who preached to me yesterday is responsible. Bring him before me at once. This is Judgment Day for him.
COUNCILLOR: Duffy the jailer! Is your prisoner still alive? The King wants to see him.
DUFFY: Coming! *(To the* GOOD CHRISTIAN.*)* Get up, you lout! I'm taking you for a walk you're not going to relish. Here

he is, sire. In God's name, grant me the privilege of carrying out his sentence.

KING: Villain, I've paid a nasty price for your sermon—my whole fortune! But your god won't be much help to you now. Duffy, I want you to think up a cruel death to destroy his body.

DUFFY: Thank you for delivering him up to me, Your Majesty. I'm going to keep him between life and death for two days before I let him give up the ghost.

GOOD CHRISTIAN: Oh King, temper your fury! Grant me respite, I beg of you, till tomorrow. Do not have me killed or tortured now! God is still in his place, and if he wishes to save me he will. One day, sire, no more time than it takes to end many a war.

KING: So be it. Leave him alone for today, Duffy, and bring him back to me tomorrow morning.

DUFFY: Back to your iron collar, vermin! May this be a week of calamities for Christians! *(He takes the GOOD CHRISTIAN back to jail.)*

GOOD CHRISTIAN: Blessed Saint Nicholas, the moment has come; I must die if you fail me now, for my enemies are mighty. A man knows his true friend in the hour of his need. Oh Lord, help your worshiper, who is sorely beset by this heathen King. He will not let me live. If the treasure is not found again I must die. Lord, help this unhappy wretch! Take pity on my fearful grief.

DUFFY: You're going to learn a painful lesson, you rascal. So much for your god and your supplication. I intend to squeeze your head in a rope full of knots.

GOOD CHRISTIAN: Help, Saint Nicholas! The enemy threatens, my time is short. Turn your eyes to me. I place myself under your unfailing protection.

ANGEL: Be still, good Christian friend, and do not lament. You will rise in triumph from your misery. Beseech Saint Nicholas and presently he will succor you. Endure your affliction without terror and do not forget Saint Nicholas, who is even now working for your deliverance. Be not discouraged: you have served him well so far. Persist in your faith, for his rain shall not leave you thirsting. Great are the rewards for those who toil in the vineyards of the Lord.

In the tavern.

SAINT NICHOLAS: Brigands, enemies of God, awake, you've slept too long, you're going to be hanged without appeal! You must come to grief for stealing the treasure, and so must the landlord for harboring it.

PINCHDICE: What's going on? Who woke us up? God, I slept like a mummy.

SAINT NICHOLAS: Whoremasters, you are all dead men. This very hour they are raising up the gallows for you. You must die for your crimes, unless you take counsel from me.

PINCHDICE: Who are you, sir, that frighten us with these terrifying words?

SAINT NICHOLAS: I am Saint Nicholas, who guides those who have lost their way. Go; you have committed a great crime; take the treasure back to the King. The image was meant to protect his coffers. Replace it at once. If your lives are dear to you, take back the treasure and place my image over it. I say no more. *(Exit.)*

PINCHDICE: Per signum sancte crucifix! What do you think of this, Clickett, and you, Razor?

RAZOR: I think he made good sense. I feel sick.

CLICKETT: Me too. Looks bad to me. I never felt so scared before.

INNKEEPER: Gentlemen, you've done a foolish piece of work. I had nothing to do with it, needless to say. Better get out of here, and on the double. I've got no taste for ill-gotten gains.

PINCHDICE: Hold on a minute. As long as we're putting our cards on the table, remember you're an accomplice. You've gotta take your fair share of the crime same as you wanted your share of the loot.

INNKEEPER: Clear out of here, sons of bitches, scum! Are you trying to discredit me? *(To* CLIP.*)* Make them pay what they owe you and then throw them out.

THE PLAY OF SAINT NICHOLAS 71

(As he leaves one way, RAZOR *and* PINCHDICE *slink off another with the sack.)*

CLIP: Come on, Mr. Clickett, don't fight it, take off your cloak. I always say, you're asking for a ruckus when you let the wrong customers in.
CLICKETT: How much do I owe?
CLIP: Sixteen dollars. Hey! Where's Razor and Pinchdice? Never mind. Your cloak will take care of yours and theirs together.
CLICKETT: You're pretty uppity all of a sudden, old Clip.
CLIP: Any complaints? Did I make a mistake in your bill? I'm doing you a favor stooping to take your cloak.
CLICKETT: Sure. When it comes to collecting you're a regular champion. *(He gives* CLIP *his cloak.)*
CLIP: And now you can go to blazes.

(Exit CLIP. CLICKETT *leaves the tavern and rejoins the other thieves in the street.)*

PINCHDICE: Gentlemen, things are going from bad to worse. The devil himself is after us and if we don't look out we'll get burned. Money comes and goes, but if they make mincemeat out of us, we ain't likely to recover. To hell with your deals, Razor.
RAZOR: All I can say is, load up again! You carried the sack out, carry it back again.
CLICKETT: My only consolation is that that blasted saloonkeeper is going to be sorry too; it's his sack we've got.
PINCHDICE: Listen, men. Nobody can call me yellow. Let's each grab a handful of these shekels. Nobody'll be the wiser, I'm telling you.
CLICKETT: Shut up, you ape! I can already feel that noose around my neck.

(They enter the Treasury.)

RAZOR: Here, set it down right here, this is where we found it. And put the image back on top.

PINCHDICE: Down you go. And curse the hour I took you up on my back.
CLICKETT: Calm down, Pinchdice, and take a fool's advice. Let's each of us go foraging our own way today. One of us is bound to succeed.
PINCHDICE: Good idea.
RAZOR: I agree. This place is too hot for us. It so happens that I've had my eye for some time on a bridal chest that I can get at without much trouble. All I have to do is break through a wall from the other side.
CLICKETT: And I'm off to Hickville, where I'm gonna give the mayor a good run for his money.
PINCHDICE: Look out for the mayor's wife, she's no fool and she'll recognize you. As far as I'm concerned, I don't want to travel, I'm too tired. There's a laundry nearby I'm gonna clean out.
RAZOR: Don't let them pinch you, Pinchdice.
PINCHDICE: God give us better luck next time.
RAZOR: So long, Clickett.
CLICKETT: So long, Razor.

(They leave.)

In the palace, next morning.

KING: Mahomet, may you give a favorable interpretation to the dream I've had, and may Tervagant too give it a happy explanation. Just as I had called my lords to a council, lo! I appeared before them with a new crown. My Lord Councillor, are you awake or asleep?
COUNCILLOR: I was asleep, sire, and having marvelous dreams. May they come true! I dreamed that the treasure had been brought back and that the thieves were hanged.
KING: Go see right away!
COUNCILLOR *(After going to the Treasury.)*: Sire, my dream didn't lie! The treasure is back and larger than before! So help me, it's grown to twice the size it was—and Saint Nicholas is lying on top of it!

KING: It can't be!

COUNCILLOR: Believe me, Your Majesty, there never was such a huge treasure. It exceeds that of Octavian, Caesar, and Hercules!

KING: Great God! What a fantastic miracle! Go fetch the Christian.

COUNCILLOR: Duffy, set the Christian gentleman free. He has nothing more to fear from you. Unlock his cell.

DUFFY (*Opening the jail.*): All right, you tramp, I was a fool not to hang you by the thumbs and pull out your molars.

COUNCILLOR: Here he is, sire. What is your pleasure—shall he live or die?

GOOD CHRISTIAN: Saint Nicholas, now preserve your faithful worshiper! Appease the anger of this King, for he has sworn to put me to death.

KING: Tell me, my Christian friend, do you really think that Saint Nicholas can help you? Do you believe he can detach me from my Law? Do you suppose he can bring me my treasure again? Are you firmly convinced of all this?

GOOD CHRISTIAN: Why not, oh King? He gave purses full of gold to three poor virgins and saved them from a life of infamy. He brought back to life three wandering students whom a criminal innkeeper had murdered. Beyond doubt he can vanquish you and make you relinquish your false religion. In him is the cause of all righteousness.

KING: Wise Christian, he has made a good beginning, for my treasure has come back to me. The miracle is evident: that which was lost has been restored. Who would have believed it possible? My good Lord Councillor, I have given my heart to Saint Nicholas, why deny it, and I shall never love another god.

COUNCILLOR: Your Majesty, I was afraid to utter my thoughts, but in my heart of hearts I reproached you for not speaking out before, because I too, like you, have begun to adore Saint Nicholas.

KING: Wise Christian, bring Saint Nicholas to me. From now on I am his humble servant.

GOOD CHRISTIAN: Oh Lord, blessed art thou for clothing this

King in grace though he stood up against thee. Verily he is a fool who doth not believe in thee and serve thee, for thy might shineth forth and striketh all eyes. King, cast away your folly now, yield your heart to God, that he may pity you, and after God worship the valiant Saint Nicholas.

DUFFY: Christian dog, I curse myself for having spared you so long.

KING: Saint Nicholas, I place myself under your protection and surrender my soul to your mercy in full and pure sincerity. I declare myself your vassal, and I renounce Apollo, Mahomet, and that vile beggar Tervagant.

COUNCILLOR: Like you, sire, I give my body and soul to the Lord Saint Nicholas. I renounce Mahomet, Apollo, their entire race and lineage, and also that stinking carcass Tervagant.

(Enter the four EMIRS.)

EMIR OF ICONIUM: Your Majesty, inasmuch as we are your vassals, we shall be converted along with you. Lords, on your knees, follow my example.

EMIR OF HYRCANIA: I give my consent.

EMIR OF OLIFERN: And so do I.

ALL THREE: Let us all be good Christians and obedient to Saint Nicholas, whose bounty has no end.

EMIR OF ARBISEK: My lords, leave me out, because I see things in a different light. I curse the man who advises me to become a renegade! You, King, better if you had choked to death when you turned perjurer and apostate. You deserve to be flayed or burned alive. From now on, I spit on your wisdom and your power. Beware of me. I defy you. I denounce my oath to you. I am no longer your vassal.

KING: To work, my lords! He'll do my pleasure like it or not. Down with him! Force him to his knees!

EMIR OF HYRCANIA: Careful, my lords, the man is strong; we'll have to take him by surprise.

EMIR OF ARBISEK: Away, you dogs! Do you think you can catch me while Mahomet protects my arms? Away, traitors, I despise you and your tricks.

EMIR OF OLIFERN: We'll make him drink at the trough all the same, because—I've got you!
EMIR OF HYRCANIA: Your Majesty, here is the traitor.
EMIR OF ARBISEK: Mercy, oh King, in the name of Mahomet, mercy! Do not make me forswear my gods! Rather behead me or let horses pull my body apart!
KING: Do as I have done! You will, you must, there's no escape.
EMIR OF ARBISEK: Saint Nicholas, I adore you under duress and against my will. Take my husk: that is all you shall have of me. My words are yours, but my true faith remains with Mahomet.

TERVAGANT: *Palas aron ozinomas*
Baske bano tudan donas
Geheamel cla orlay
Berek he pantaras tay.

GOOD CHRISTIAN: What did Tervagant say, your Majesty?
KING: He is dying of grief and rage because I turned to the true God. But I don't care about his speeches now. Toss him out of his synagogue, my friend.
COUNCILLOR: Tervagant, you are about to experience to your grief the prophetic meaning of your laughter and tears. Come tumbling down from your pedestal, you empty bladder! Down from your eminence! Sire, I have given him a good mauling.
KING: Now, wise Christian, we shall get ourselves baptized at once. My only boast from now on is this: I am the servant of the Lord.
GOOD CHRISTIAN: Let us all together sing the glory of God: *Te Deum laudamus.*

HERE ENDS THE PLAY OF SAINT NICHOLAS
WHICH JEHANS BODIAUS WROUGHT. AMEN.

The Play of Robin and Marion

(LE JEU DE ROBIN ET MARION)

by Adam de la Halle

Two generations after Jean Bodel, Arras was still thriving. An oligarchy of plutocrats shared power with the King of France, the Count of Artois, the bishop, and the local abbots of St. Vaast, lent money to these and other powerful men, sent their textiles as far as the Orient, quarreled over taxes and privileges, and patronized artists like so many Italians. The literary society of which Bodel had been a member prospered along with the rest of the town. Its members continued to busy themselves with processions, banquets, poetic contests, debates, songs, plays, practical jokes, and religious duties to the totemic candle. The rolls show that some of the richest and most influential men of Arras belonged to the *puy* at that time.

Among the one hundred eighty-two professional minstrels whose names the records of thirteenth-century Arras have preserved, the most famous is Adam de la Halle, also known by the family sobriquet of le Bossu. He was born around the middle of the century, the son of a minor civil servant in town. Well-to-do citizens helped the boy obtain a good education at a nearby Cistercian monastery. When Bodel returned to Arras, he probably became a member of the *puy*, and may have begun to take part in local politics on the side of his wealthy patrons. Although we know of no source of income for the poet-musician in these years other than purses and dinners from amateurs of the better things of life, it must be remembered that the record of Adam's life consists, as is to be expected, mostly of gaps.

Presently Adam fell in love with a beautiful girl as poor as himself, and for her sake he delayed for several years the long journey to higher studies at the Sorbonne. Shortly after they were married, he did set out for Paris, however, and before his departure he entertained the *puy* with a unique Aristophanic "revue" entitled *Le Jeu de la Feuillée*—not a play, really, but a great deal of romping, chatting, bantering about himself, his wife, his father, the citizens of Arras, a few of the issues of the day, along with a little hexing and witching and a volley of gags. This extremely topical skit yields much of the information we have about Adam and his family. It is as sprightly, casual, and easygoing as the later *Robin and Marion*, utterly formless (this is not necessarily a vice), but unfortunately buried for us under the footnotes that make it intelligible.

The records show no evidence that his studies in Paris brought Adam any tangible benefits. Back in Arras, he seems to have become entangled in the resistance of its wealthy citizens to a special tax that Louis IX was levying for yet another crusade. We are now in 1270, four crusades after the one that had apparently aroused Bodel's enthusiasm. By this time tempers had cooled, the rich citizens were skeptical, they grumbled, cheated, and were finally exiled for a few years. Adam, who must have been one of their pamphleteers, departed with them and settled in Douai, a few miles away. As it turned out, the Eighth Crusade came to an abrupt end with the death of Saint Louis before Tunis.

In 1271 Philip III was crowned. That same year he visited Arras, where he received a splendid four-day welcome. It was probably on this occasion that the exiles were pardoned and returned. In 1272 Adam's stock rose dramatically when the Count of Artois—nephew to Saint Louis, heroic crusader, and patron of the arts—took him into his household. The age distinguished sharply between the itinerant and rain-soaked minstrel at one end of the spectrum and the liveried lute-playing servant of a lord at the other. Adam had never been a vagabond—far from it, for he counted the "best people" of Arras as his patrons—but he had now taken a considerable step upward. His new position gave him a fixed income, official and many unofficial perquisites, and prestige.

The King of Naples and Sicily in these years was another uncle of the count's, Charles of Anjou, a brave and bloody tyrant. When the Sicilians massacred the French during the famous Vespers of 1282, the count rushed to his uncle's aid, accompanied by his entire household, minstrels included. In Naples, Adam apparently passed for a time into the service of Charles himself, and sang fulsome praises of his brutal master in an unfinished epic called *The King of Sicily*—a flattering title, for Sicily was lost. Charles was rapidly turning Naples into a French city. There, sometime in the eighties, amidst barbarous plots and slaughters, attacks and revenges, war and preparation for war, Adam composed and undoubtedly produced the idyllic eclogue of *Robin and Marion*. The retinues of king and count were probably charmed and perhaps moved by these peaceful scenes of faraway France. But *Robin and Marion* proved to be Adam's last major work. He died around 1287 or 1288. According to one story, the faithful Count of Artois (who had become regent after the death of Charles) would take visitors to see the poet's tomb in Naples. In or around 1290, the play was performed in Arras itself in what seems to have been an extraordinary celebration in Adam's honor.

Robin and Marion appears to have remained in the northern French repertory for a century or two. Thereafter it vanishes from history, to emerge again in the early nineteenth century when the first edition was printed. Three manuscripts survive, two of which give much of the music for the play. Beyond this, we have from Adam's hand a variety of songs, poetic games, trifles, a couple of sententious poems on Love and Death, and—emulating Bodel—a fine *Farewell* to the city of Arras. But today as in the Middle Ages, his fame rests chiefly on the *Jeu de Robin et Marion*.

Adam le Bossu did not invent the personages of Robin and Marion, the little incident with the knight, and the bucolic entertainment that follows. A straight line of descent leads us to him from Theocritus and Vergil. In Adam's own day, the narrative versified *pastourelle* was a familiar literary and musical genre. But when Adam converted narration into drama, he did so with an inimitable gracefulness, nonchalance, and good-natured innocence—the innocence, it goes without saying, of a clever professional. The play is as insubstantial as dew, but it is given to few writers to be both insubstantial and ingratiating. And even in a prose version, Adam ingratiates himself.

The traditional *pastourelle* tended to be coarse. Either the knight satisfies his appetite and makes a fool of Robin, or Robin mauls the knight with a stick. Usually the peasants end with a wild free-for-all, broken jaws, and bloody noses. All this changes under Adam's management. The knight withdraws of his own volition with face-saving disdain; the girl preserves her virtue and proves her fidelity; Robin shows himself a doughty wolf-fighter after a little vexation with the knight; and the villagers, though now and then a bit raw, conclude the day with a dance rather than a brawl. "Adam," says his nineteenth-century biographer, "has had the talent to draw from his models only what was sunny and delicate in them." A few gross remarks in the mouth of Pighead Simon serve only to increase the sense of refinement we get from the play, for they are immediately rebuked by the stern little Marion and re-proved—more, we guess, for her sake than for his own—by the devoted Robin. Through Simon, too, Adam succeeds in making his idyll credible, for he keeps it in touch with the earth.

The same credibility results from the natural sprightliness of the language, the unassuming chitchat, the down-to-earth concerns. We are happily distant from the inflated world of the Renaissance, where artists summarily killed the medieval simplicities and would not venture into the sun without their ample "mantle of learning." Adam's villagers do not speak in Ciceronian periods, they do not allude to the classics, they know no ingenious similes. This is not, in other words, the pastoral of Guarini, Fletcher, or Lope de Vega.

Credibility is not inconsistent with escapism. Adam has created an escapist playlet for the Neapolitan garrison, but he has done this not by making fantastic creatures out of his shepherds, but, altogether differently, by eliminating evil and reconciling conflicts for these otherwise real creatures. It is a censoring out, not a transmogrifying. If the result is a trifle anemic—think of the luscious and passionate world of *Daphnis and Chloe!*—this is as much as saying that Adam, for all his gifts, is but one of the minor immortals.

The point of view is strictly patrician. The line into the past takes us back to Theocritus, but the line into the future leads to Marie Antoinette's rustic *hameau* in the shadow of the palace at Versailles. For even though Adam likes his lads and lasses, he makes children of them. True, he might be thought to be saying to his audience, "How lovely it is to be like a child," and again, "How delightful it is to be content with bread, cheese, and plain water," but nothing really serious can be made of this; the lads and lasses live in too simple a world, and they are too simpleminded, to impress a serious pastoral message on the minds of Charles's courtiers and soldiers. Children they remain. Adam makes no propaganda for the bucolic life.

As a form, Adam's play must admit to a few venial sins. It breaks rather too obviously into two parts: the encounter with the knight, and the picnic and games. Once the knight is gone, he is forgotten. The play is in effect a brief drama followed by a long nondramatic divertissement in the form of a coda, where the tail in question is longer than the body. This formal weakness is not very disturbing, however, for the play flows smoothly and naturally on. After the danger, it says, let us refresh ourselves with games.

A genuine weak spot occurs when the knight abruptly releases Marion. After building up to a climax, Adam cheats us and dissolves the action. This is not "medieval naïveté"—medieval playwrights knew better. We may agree with Henri Guy, who supposes that Adam wanted to give Robin the victory, but was unwilling, before a noble audience, to humiliate the knight. His solution was to duck the whole problem.

Like most medieval plays, this one lacks "due time." Although the dialogue is sprightly and sophisticated, it also tends to jump from one subject to another without transition. Bodel had done much better with a more difficult action. But not until we come to *Pathelin*, to *Everyman*, and to the *Celestina* —two centuries later—do we find playwrights regularly attentive to due time. Our only defense for the deficiency is that the actor can more or less overcome it in performance.

In the creation of character, Adam did what needed to be done: a touch here, a suggestion there. The eclogue is no place for psychology. Robin is a likable lad with a tiny fault or two. He adores Marion; he is a fine musician and a famous dancer; and he is incapable of malice. Marion is amorous, but chastened by a strong feeling for the proprieties. This is a particularly delightful invention of Adam's. Perhaps he endowed his little heroine with some of the virtues he had found in his wife. Marion is courageous and tender, lively but organized. Her primness only enhances the gifts she keeps for her lover when they will be alone. Here the finesse that Marivaux and Musset will perpetuate appears already in all its tenuous glory.

Among the other participants, only Simon stands out with his contrasting roughness. Harry carries with him the merest hint of kinship with O'Casey's Joxer. The others, including the knight, are not characterized in any way.

Was the play performed outdoors? The presence of a horse —a horse that gallops off—would seem to indicate that it was. And if not—it should have been. It is such a breezy play, so green, so fresh, so full of leaves and grass, birds and lambs, and apples and cheese, that it is hard to visualize inside four walls and under artificial lights. But outdoors or indoors, we have before us the usual multiple stage of the Middle Ages, where a few steps taken by an actor lead us from meadow to village, and from village to wood.

The play should not be read without the sound of music in our ears and the sight of dancers in our imagination. *Robin and Marion* is our first musical comedy, just as it is very nearly the first fully secular play extant in medieval Europe. We know, however, that Adam did not compose either the lyrics or the music for his play. He used popular songs wherever he found an opening for them, and perhaps he even built his playlet with such songs especially in mind, for now and then he seems to give the conversation a twist for no other apparent reason than to introduce a familiar tune. As a result, *Robin and Marion* is incidentally a precious anthology of thirteenth-century popular music.

I have made no attempt to translate these songs. It would take a reckless man to try to render into merry and acceptable English

> Hé! Robeçon,
> Leure leure va.
> Car vien a moi,
> Leure leure va.
> S'irons jüer
> Du leure leure va,
> Du leure leure va.

Instead, I have devised songs that remain, I hope, within the spirit of the originals without being in themselves disgraceful. Nor have I followed the metrical schemes of the originals so as to fit my words to the musical score. If the present version is to be staged, it will require new music.

My text for this translation is that published by Albert Pauphilet in *Jeux et Sapience du Moyen Âge* (Paris: Gallimard, Bibl. de la Pléiade, 1951).

BIBLIOGRAPHY

FRANK, GRACE. *The Medieval French Drama*. Oxford, 1954. Chapter XXII. This is the only genuine account of Adam's work in English, and fortunately it is excellent.

GUY, HENRI. *Essai sur la vie et les oeuvres littéraires du trouvère Adam de le Hale*. Paris, 1898. This is the exhaustive work on Adam.

DE COUSSEMAKER, E. *Oeuvres de Adam de la Halle*. Paris, 1872. This contains the musical score for the play.

For those who want an English text that can be sung to the original music, there is a somewhat cut and bowdlerized yet graceful translation by J. Murray Gibbon in *The Play of Robin and Marion*, a Schirmer piano score of the medieval music "reconstructed and harmonized in the manner of the period" by Jean Beck (New York, 1928).

JONES, WILLIAM P. *The Pastourelle*. Princeton, 1930. A general work on the *pastourelle*.

An excellent recording of the music, based on the manuscript sources, was made in 1966 by the Early Music Quartet for Telefunken (Cat. No. SAWT 9504-AEx).

THE PLAY OF ROBIN AND MARION

CHARACTERS

Robin
Marion
A Knight
Pighead Simon
Walter
Alice
Harry
Two Fiddlers

A meadow.

MARION *(Singing and weaving a garland.)*:
>Robin loves me,
>>Why should I say no?
>
>Bought me once a pretty belt,
>Bought me twice a pretty bow,
>Sang to me the love he felt,
>Kissed me hard and kissed me deep,
>>So why should I say no?
>>And why should Robin weep?

KNIGHT *(On horseback, singing.)*:
>The joust was done,
>The fight was won,
>And as I rode I saw a lass,
>A flower sitting in the springtime grass. . . .

MARION *(Singing.)*:
>Summer joy and winter bliss,
>Robin loves me, I am his.

KNIGHT: Good morning in God's name, my lovely.
MARION: Good morning, my lord.
KNIGHT: Tell me, sweetheart, why it is you're singing so happily,
  Summer joy and winter bliss,
  Robin loves me, I am his.
MARION: My handsome lord, I'm singing for a very good reason. I am in love with Robin, Robin is in love with me. And to prove how much he loves me, he has given me this basket, my shepherd's crook, and a fine sharp knife.
KNIGHT: Have you seen any birds flying over these fields, my dear?
MARION: I have, my lord, I don't know how many. And here in this hedge you can hear the linnets and the goldfinches whistling merrily away.
KNIGHT: I meant wild geese, not songbirds, my lovely. And have you seen any pheasants by the river?
MARION: Peasants? Oh yes, I saw three of them on this road yesterday, carrying heavy sacks to the mill. Does that answer your question?
KNIGHT: Beautifully! What about herons, my dear?
MARION: Herrings, my lord? Not a single one, on my soul, not since Lent, when my grandmother Emma was serving them at table. These are my grandmother's sheep, by the way.
KNIGHT: I'm speechless! The girl is making a fool of me.
MARION: My lord, what sort of beast is that on your fist?
KNIGHT: It's a falcon.
MARION: Does it like bread?
KNIGHT: No, only meat.
MARION: Really? A beast with a leather head that likes meat![1] But where are you going?
KNIGHT: To the meadow beyond.
MARION: I must say, Robin is better company than you. When he plays the bagpipe he fills the village with noise from one end to the other.

[1] The falcon's head was covered with a hood.

THE PLAY OF ROBIN AND MARION

KNIGHT: Tell me, my angel, could you fall in love with a noble knight?
MARION: Step back, my lord. I don't know what a knight is. Of all men alive, I'll never love anyone except Robin. Morning and evening he comes to me and brings me bread and cheese. Look, here's a piece left in my basket.[2]
KNIGHT: And yet, my lovely, wouldn't it be fine to ride with me into the wood and play a delightful game with me?
MARION: My lord! Take your horse away! He almost hurt me. Robin's horse doesn't rear when I follow his plow.
KNIGHT: Be my sweetheart, shepherd girl; give in to me, do.
MARION: Leave me, sir. It's not right for you to remain here. What is your name?
KNIGHT: Aubrey.
MARION *(Sings.)*:
    No use, Aubrey my lord,
        Robin is my lover's name;
    Farewell, Aubrey my lord,
        Hunt another game.
KNIGHT: Is it really no?
MARION: Really no.
KNIGHT: Is loving me beneath your dignity, that you won't listen to my prayer? Remember, I am a nobleman, you are a shepherdess.
MARION: That will never make me love you. I'm a country lass, but I've a friend who is handsome, charming, and merry.
KNIGHT: God give you pleasure with him, shepherd girl. Since it can't be helped, my lips are sealed, and I'm on my way.

(He sings.)

    Folderol, folderol, diddle-di-hey,
    Oh as I was riding out a wood,

---

[2] In her bosom, in the original, where the girl would normally carry things, for pockets did not exist as yet. I have sought to avoid either the leer or the giggle, both of which would be untrue to the original at this point.

Didn't I see a lass, comely and gay,
A queen might envy her, how proud she stood,
Folderol, folderol, diddle-di-hey,
How proud, how delicate, how gay.

(He rides away.)

MARION *(Sings.)*:
  Robin Robin
    Come to me
  Tarry-larry-lo;
  Robin Robin
  Play with me
  Tarry-larry-lo.
ROBIN *(Off-stage, singing.)*:
  Mary Mary
    Come to me
  Tarry-larry-lo;
  Mary Mary
  Play with me
  Tarry-larry-lo.
MARION: Robin!
ROBIN *(Entering.)*: Marion!
MARION: Where have you been?
ROBIN: I went to put on my heavy jacket because of the cold. And I've brought you some apples. Here they are.
MARION: I could tell at a distance that it was you singing. And how did you know it was me?
ROBIN: By your voice, too, and I recognized the sheep.
MARION: You don't know what happened, my love, and I don't want you to take it amiss. A man on horseback came by; he had a pair of mittens on, and carried a mean-looking bird on his fist. He wanted to make love to me, but he didn't succeed, because I'll never be false to you.
ROBIN: You would have been the death of me, Marion. If only I'd got here a bit sooner, along with cousin Walter and Pighead Simon, you would have seen a brawl fit for the devil.
MARION: Please don't lose your temper, dear. Let's have a snack on the grass, just you and me.

ROBIN: Do I have to stand and serve you, or get down on my knees?
MARION: Sit down next to me, silly, and eat with me.
ROBIN: You don't have to ask me twice. But I didn't bring anything along, wretch that I am.
MARION: Don't worry. Here's some cheese left, here's a solid piece of bread, and here are the apples you brought me.
ROBIN: Lovely fat cheese! Here, my little bird, eat.
MARION: You too. Tell me when you're ready for a sip of water. This pitcher is our fountain.
ROBIN: If only we had a few strips of your grandmother's bacon!
MARION: That's not for us, Robin. She has it hanging out of our reach. Let's be happy with what we have; it's enough for this morning.
ROBIN: God, my bones still ache from the wrestling I did on the green the other day.[3]
MARION *(Admiringly.)*: Did you wrestle, really?
ROBIN *(Singing.)*:
    So the tale is told,
    Love, so the tale is told.
MARION: Don't you want to eat anymore?
ROBIN: No, thank you, dear.
MARION: Then I'll put the rest away until we're hungry again. Now ask me anything you like, and I'll obey you.
ROBIN: Good. I'm going to test you to see whether you're as true to me as I am to you. *(He sings.)*
    Round in a whirl,
    My sweetest girl,
  Give me the garland you made,
  Give me the garland you made.
MARION *(Singing.)*:
    I shall set it in your hair,
      But will you care,
    Will you love me if I do?
    Will you love me if I do?

[3] In the original, Robin reports that he has played a game of *choule*, a sort of field hockey popular among villagers and known to be particularly rough.

ROBIN *(Singing.)*:
>I will love you if you do,
>Give you ribbons pink and blue,
>>Then a collar for your breast,
>>And a white skirt for the rest.
>>>So round in a whirl,
>>>My sweetest girl,
>>Give me the garland you made.

MARION *(Singing.)*: Here it is every flower and blade.
And now I want you to dance for me.
ROBIN: Which dance do you like best? Everybody knows that I can do them all.

Song and Dance

MARION:
>Robin, by your father's soul,
>Can you foot it well?

ROBIN:
>Watch me, by my mother's soul,
>See how I excel,
>>Front and back
>And back to front and front and back.

MARION:
>Robin, by your father's soul,
>Can you shake your head?

ROBIN:
>Watch me, by my mother's soul,
>My rivals have all fled,
>>Left and right
>And right to left and left and right.

MARION:
>Robin, by your father's soul,
>Can you fling your arms?

ROBIN:
>Watch me, by my mother's soul,
>You'll praise me for my charms.
>>Up and down
>And down and up and up and down.

MARION: Say, Robin, do you know how to lead a morris dance?
ROBIN: I do, but the earth is too soft, and my shoes are torn.
MARION: Never mind. We're dressed as well as we need to be. Go on, Robin.
ROBIN: Wait, I'll go fetch my drum and bagpipe. And I'll call Simon if I can find him, and Walter too. Besides, they'll be useful if the rider comes back.
MARION: Don't be long, Robin, and if you see my friend Alice on the way, invite her too, she's very good company. You'll find her back of the gardens on the way to the mill. And now hurry up.
ROBIN: I'll roll up my trousers and run all the way.
MARION: Go now.

(ROBIN *runs to the village.*)

ROBIN: Simon, Walter, are you home? Open the door!
SIMON: It's good to see you, Robin. But why are you out of breath?
ROBIN: Why am I out of breath? Don't ask! I can hardly talk.
WALTER: Did someone give you a beating?
ROBIN: Certainly not!
SIMON: Let us know if anybody's injured you.
ROBIN: Listen to me, both of you. A while ago a rascal on horseback tried to seduce my little Marion. I don't know who he was, but I'm afraid he'll return, and so I want you both to come with me.
WALTER: If he tries again, he'll be sorry.
SIMON: Sorry's not the word!
ROBIN: Besides, if you come along we'll have a bit of fun all together—you, us, Harry, and Alice. There'll be plenty of bread, first-rate cheese, and clean water.
WALTER: Lead the way, my boy.
ROBIN: You two walk ahead while I go look for Harry and Alice.
WALTER: Good. You go your way and we'll go ours. I'm taking my strongest pitchfork along.

SIMON: And I've got this nail-studded club.

(They leave.)

ROBIN: Alice! Alice!
ALICE: Is that you, Robin? What news?
ROBIN: You don't know. Marion wants you to come and dance and play with us in the field.
ALICE: Who'll be there?
ROBIN: Me and you; then Pighead Simon, Walter, Harry, and Marion.
ALICE: Shall I change into my Sunday skirt?
ROBIN: Oh no, you're beautiful in the one you're wearing. Hurry up and follow me.
ALICE: I will, as soon as I've gathered my sheep together.

Each goes his way. MARION *reappears in the meadow. Then the* KNIGHT *enters; he is without his falcon, but a few dead birds hang from his saddle.*

KNIGHT: Say, shepherd girl, aren't you the one I met this morning?
MARION: On your way, my lord, for God's sake!
KNIGHT: I mean no harm. I'm only looking for my falcon; it flew away.
MARION: I saw it flying over the hedge a minute ago. You'll surely find it if you follow in that direction.
KNIGHT: Are you telling the truth?
MARION: Oh yes!
KNIGHT: Of course, the bird wouldn't matter to me if I had a sweetheart like you.
MARION: For the love of God, leave me, my lord. I'm frightened!
KNIGHT: Why?
MARION: Because of Robin.
KNIGHT: Because of Robin?
MARION: Yes. If he knew—he'd stop loving me—and he's everything I have.
KNIGHT: You needn't fear anyone if you'll listen to me.

THE PLAY OF ROBIN AND MARION

MARION: My lord, somebody will come and see us together. Go away, please! Let me be. I've nothing to say to you. I must take care of my flock.

KNIGHT: I'm a fool to stay here matching wits with you.

MARION: You must go away now! I hear people coming!

KNIGHT: Farewell, my sweet; I won't use force on you. *(He rides away, but meets* ROBIN *who has found the falcon.)* Hey, you rascal, don't murder my falcon! You're asking for a lump on your head!

ROBIN: That would be unjust, my lord; I'm trying to keep the bird from escaping.

KNIGHT: Take this! *(He cuffs* ROBIN.*)* It's your pay for handling him so gently.

ROBIN: Help! People! Help!

KNIGHT: Here's something else for making so much noise. *(He cuffs* ROBIN *again.)*

MARION *(At a distance.)*: Mother of God! That's Robin shouting! Somebody must have attacked him. I can't leave my flock—but he's in danger—never mind the sheep! Oh dear, it's the knight! He must have struck Robin because of me. Robin, love, what happened?

ROBIN: He's killed me, that's all.

MARION: God punish you, my lord; you've torn his clothes to shreds.

KNIGHT: See how he mauled my falcon!

MARION: He doesn't know how to handle it; it's not his fault. You must pardon him.

KNIGHT: Very gladly—if you'll come away with me.

MARION: Never!

KNIGHT: We'll see about that. It's you I want, and nobody else will do. Up on my horse and away!

MARION: Robin! Robin! He's carrying me off! Why don't you help me?

(The KNIGHT *rides away with* MARION.*)*

ROBIN: Oh misery! I've lost everything! My cousins will have arrived too late! I've lost Marion, I've taken a beating, and my clothes are torn to bits!

SIMON *(Off-stage, singing.)*:
> Shepherd get up, why are you sleeping?
> Where you have sown, another is reaping!

ROBIN: Simon, Walter, is that you? I've lost everything—Marion is gone!

SIMON: Let's rescue her!

ROBIN: Are you mad? He'd massacre five hundred of us. This horseman is a demon. I wish you'd seen the huge sword he was flashing about! He gave me a blow I'll feel for a year.

SIMON: There would have been a scrap if I'd come on time.

ROBIN: Let's find out where they galloped off—by lying in wait behind these bushes. With your help I'll rescue her. My courage is almost coming back.

(They leave.)

(Enter MARION *and the* KNIGHT.*)*

MARION: Leave me, my lord, it's the wisest thing to do.

KNIGHT: By no means, my pretty; I am taking you with me, and you shall have from me—you know what. Why so proud? Here's a gift for you: a river fowl that I killed; it will be your dinner tonight.

MARION: I prefer my rich cheese, my bread, and plain apples to your fancy dishes. You can't do anything I shall ever like, my lord.

KNIGHT: Nothing at all that would please you?

MARION: Nothing, nothing at all.

KNIGHT: Well, I am a fool for bothering with this silly creature. Farewell, shepherd girl.

MARION: Farewell, sir knight.

(He leaves.)

MARION: Poor Robin, he must be in a terrible state, thinking he has lost me.

ROBIN *(Offstage.)*: Hello! Hello!

MARION: Oh my God, it's Robin calling! Robin, how is it with you?

(Enter ROBIN, SIMON, *and* WALTER.)

ROBIN: I'm happy and my fever is gone now that I see you again.
MARION: Let me hug you.
ROBIN: Come here. *(He kisses her.)*
MARION: Look at the fool kissing me in front of people!
WALTER: We're all cousins, Marion; don't be shy before us.
MARION: I don't mind in front of you, but he's such a little fool, he'd do it in the middle of the village.
ROBIN: I certainly would! *(He kisses her again.)*
MARION: Again! Isn't he a lion!
ROBIN: God, if that knight came back now, I'd raise a storm!
MARION: I believe you, Robin, but what's the use? You don't even know how I managed to escape.
ROBIN: Oh yes, I do; we all saw how you handled him. And ask Walter—ask Simon—how they had to hold me down when I saw you snatched away. Three times I tore myself from their grip.
SIMON: Robin, you're a genuine hero; but now that it's all over, better forget it.
ROBIN: Harry and Alice should be coming soon. Oh, here they are!
MARION: You're right!
ROBIN: Harry, you brought your bagpipe!
HARRY: Yes, I did.
MARION: I'm so glad to see you, Alice.
ALICE: And I'm pleased to see you, Marion.
MARION: You don't know how much I missed you. Now we can sing,
 Here's a merry jolly crowd,
 No one surly, no one proud.
WALTER: Are we all present?
HARRY: Yes.
MARION: Let's think of a game to play.
HARRY: How about Kings and Queens?
MARION: I prefer the games we play at Christmastime, when the gifts are opened.

HARRY: How about "Who laughs first"?
MARION: Oh I don't like all that laughing.
HARRY: Well, Marion, you be careful to keep a straight face.
MARION: What are the rules?
HARRY: One of us plays Saint Damian.[4] The others have to bring the saint an offering, one by one. Whoever laughs first forfeits his offering and has to take the place of the saint.
SIMON: Who'll be the saint?
ROBIN: Me.
WALTER: Agreed. Simon, you bring the first offering.
SIMON: Here is an offering, Saint Damian. And if that's not enough, here's something more.[5]
ROBIN: Ha! He laughed!
SIMON: It's true. *(He takes Robin's place.)*
WALTER: Your turn, Marion.
MARION: Who lost?
WALTER: Simon.
MARION: Here is a gift, sweet saint.
WALTER: Watch how she's controlling herself. Fine. Alice is next.
ALICE: Handsome saint, please accept this present.
ROBIN: Not bad; you didn't crack a smile. Walter is next, and then Harry.
WALTER: Here's a fine present, Saint Damian.
SIMON: You're laughing, you lose too.
WALTER: I didn't laugh!
SIMON: Never mind then. Harry next.
HARRY: My turn. Here are two coins for you.
SIMON: You lose!
HARRY: Gently, gently, I haven't laughed yet.
SIMON: What's that? Are you splitting hairs with me? Some-

---

[4] Saint Cosmas in the original. Saints Cosmas and Damian were twins who practiced medicine without asking for fees in order to make converts for Christianity; hence they were known as "moneyless." I have used the other twin because the modern audience is apt to hear "cosmos" instead of "Cosmas."

[5] We are to assume that both he and the "saint" now make faces at each other. As for the nature of the "offerings," the text gives no information aside from the coins mentioned a few lines down.

body's looking for a bloody nose. Pay up and don't make trouble.

HARRY: All right, I will.

ROBIN: Is peace restored, Saint Damian?

MARION: Stop, everybody; this is a nasty game. Don't you agree, Alice?

ALICE: It's a stupid game. Let's think of something else. What can we play at? We're two girls and four lads.

SIMON: Why don't we see who can let out the loudest poop? That's what I call fun.

ROBIN: I won't stand for indecent talk in front of my Marion, do you hear? It may be fun for some, but don't let it happen again.

SIMON: Anything for the sake of peace.

WALTER: Well, what game shall we play?

HARRY: What do you propose?

WALTER: Both Simon and me want to play "Catch the Liar." I'll ask sharp questions if you'll make me king.

HARRY: No sir, the king has to be picked.

SIMON: Well said, brother. Whoever is number ten gets to be king.

HARRY: Everybody agreed? Very good. Out with your hands.

WALTER: Who'll start?

HARRY: Simon.

SIMON: All right. One.

HARRY: Two.

ROBIN: Three.

WALTER: Four.

HARRY: Your turn, Marion.

MARION: Five.[6]

ALICE: Six.

SIMON: Seven.

HARRY: Eight.

ROBIN: Nine.

WALTER: Ten. I'm king!

SIMON: I don't think anyone can object.

---

[6] This is the second time we find Marion distracted and inattentive. Is she flirting with Robin? Mending her bow?

ROBIN: Let's raise him high and crown him. There! That's good.
HARRY: Wait. Alice, instead of a crown, give him your straw hat.
ALICE: Here, your majesty.
WALTER: I summon thee, Pighead Simon, to the throne.
SIMON: I am all obedience, sire; command me to do anything I like, I shall perform it for you at once.
WALTER: Tell me then: hast thou ever been jealous?
SIMON: I have, your majesty; I became jealous of a dog that I heard scratching at my girl friend's door the other day. I thought it was a man.
WALTER: Robin, thou art next.
ROBIN: Welcome, king, and ask me anything you wish.
WALTER: Robin, when an animal is born, how dost thou know whether it be male or female?
ROBIN: That's what I call an interesting question.
WALTER: Answer it then.
ROBIN: No, I won't. But if your majesty wishes to find out, he has only to lift the animal's tail and look underneath. I'll say nothing else. You're trying to make me blush.
MARION: He's right!
WALTER: Is this any concern of thine?
MARION: Yes, it is, because it's an improper question.
WALTER: Well then, Marion, I want him to express a wish.
ROBIN: I don't dare, sire.
WALTER: Oh no? Go thou and embrace Marion in such wise as to please her.

(ROBIN *kisses* MARION.)

MARION: No kissing, you good-for-nothing!
ROBIN: I didn't kiss anybody!
MARION: Oh the liar! You can still see the mark. Look—I think he bit my cheek.
ROBIN: I felt you so soft and tender, I thought I was nibbling at fresh cheese. Come into my arms and make up.
MARION: Go away, you devil, you're as heavy as a log.
ROBIN: And you're mean to me.

MARION: Come here and don't be cross. I won't say another word. Don't be unhappy.
WALTER: Harry, stand thou before me.
HARRY: I will, sire, if such is your wish.
WALTER: Tell us, Harry, and may God be kind to thy soul, what is thy favorite repast? I shall know if thou failest to tell the truth.
HARRY: Your majesty, I love best a fat and heavy backside of pork with a strong mash of nuts and garlic. I ate so much of it last week that I had to run all day.
WALTER: Harry is always predictable.
HARRY: It's your turn, Alice.
ALICE: I'd rather not.
WALTER: Alice, come here. Tell me, as thou art loyal to me, what is the greatest delight of love thou didst ever enjoy in any place whatsoever. Speak. I am listening.
ALICE: With pleasure. I enjoy most when a certain man, who has devoted to me his heart and his body, comes to keep me company near my sheep, without doing any evil, of course, and as often as possible.
WALTER: Without doing any evil?
ALICE: It's the truth.
HARRY: She's fibbing!
WALTER: Very likely. Now to Marion. Come along, appear before the throne.
MARION: I want a respectable question.
WALTER: Gladly. Tell me, little Marion, how much thou lovest that handsome scamp, my cousin Robin. And a curse fall on thee if thou liest.
MARION: I won't lie. I love him with so much love that I love him more than any of my sheep, even the one that had a lamb.
WALTER: That, by God, is what I call passion. Let the world take example.
SIMON *(Crying out.)*: Marion! Trouble! A wolf is running away with one of your sheep!
MARION: Robin, run, before the wolf eats it!
ROBIN *(To* SIMON.*)*: Lend me your club—you'll see whether

I'm brave or not. Harrow! Harrow! The wolf! The wolf! *(He vanishes, and presently returns carrying a sheep in his arms.)* Here, Marion, now you can decide whether I've any courage.

MARION: Poor little thing! It's hurt all over!

ROBIN: See how muddy it became.

MARION: You're holding the poor thing with its little behind squeezed against its head.

ROBIN: I was in a hurry, that's why. Feel where the wolf caught it with his teeth.

SIMON: And look how blue it is *here*.

MARION: Dirty fellow!

ROBIN: Take it, Marion. And watch out for its teeth!

MARION: With all that mud on its fleece? I don't want it. Let it down to graze.

WALTER: Now, Robin, listen to me. If you love Marion as much as you seem to, I'd advise you to take her to you, provided Simon gives his consent.

SIMON: I give my consent.

ROBIN: Is this all mine?

MARION: Robin! You're squeezing me too hard! Can't you do it gently?

WALTER: I'm surprised that Alice isn't tempted when she sees these two.

ALICE: Who? Me? Tempted? I don't know any man who ever cared for me.

WALTER: There might be one, who knows? If you were bold enough to try him.

ALICE: Who for instance?

WALTER: Me, or Simon.

HARRY: Better try me, my pigeon.

SIMON: You? Why you? For the sake of your bagpipe? That's the only treasure you can call your own. I, on the other hand, own a strong draft horse with a good harness, a plough, and a harrow. I'm the richest man in my street. My overcoat matches the rest of my clothes. My mother has a precious tankard that will fall to me when she dies, a sack of grain a month for a windmill she sold, and a cow that provides us with all the milk and cheese we need. Doesn't that make me a good catch?

ALICE: It does. But I won't take a chance because of my brother John and you both. You're two fools, and you'd keep me from gadding about the way I enjoy. It would be war every day.

SIMON: Well, I don't care whether you want me or not. Let's settle the other wedding first.

HARRY *(To* ALICE.): What's in your satchel?

ALICE: Bread, salt, and watercress. What have you got, Marion?

MARION: Robin knows. We have this morning's leftovers—bread, cheese, and the apples he brought me. Here they are, they're for everybody.

SIMON: Who'd like two salted hams?

HARRY: Where are they?

SIMON *(Producing them.)*: Not very far.

WALTER: And I brought two fresh pieces of cheese.

HARRY: What kind?

ALICE: They're goat cheese.

ROBIN: I've got some roasted peas.

HARRY: Is that the best you can do? You won't get away with it![7]

ROBIN: Wait. I also have a few baked apples. Would you like some, Marion?

MARION: Is that all?

ROBIN: No.

MARION: Tell me the truth. What have you really kept for me?

ROBIN *(Sings.)*:
    A lamb pie just for you,
    Luscious through and through—
      Then give me the tip
      Of your cherry-red lip,
    And that, sweet Marion, will suffice
      For paradise.
Would you like more?

MARION: Yes!

---

[7] However, Harry does not seem to have anything at all to offer. Perhaps Simon was right about him.

ROBIN: I'll bring you—*(Sings.)*
   A capon on a plate,
   Fattest in the state—
      Then give me the tip
      Of your cherry-red lip,
   And that, sweet Marion, will suffice
      For paradise.
I'll hurry home and bring everything here.
MARION: Hurry back.
ROBIN: I will, love; but don't wait for me, fall to while I'm gone.
MARION: That would be unfair. I'm going to wait for you.
ROBIN: Why not take off your apron; stretch it on the grass like a tablecloth, and put all the foodstuff on it. I'll be back in no time at all. *(He leaves.)*
MARION: Let's use your apron, Alice, because it's whiter than mine.
ALICE: If you want to. There. Stretch it out where you think best.
HARRY: Everybody put his contribution down.
ALICE: Look Marion, I think I see Robin coming back.
MARION: Yes, it's Robin, and he's dancing! Isn't he a darling? What do you think of him?
ALICE: He's a fine boy, and he does his best to please you.
MARION: Look at the two fiddlers he's brought along![8]
HARRY: Where?
SIMON: Can't you see the two fellows with him?
HARRY: Yes, yes, I see them now!

(Enter ROBIN and the fiddlers.)

ROBIN: I'm back, Marion. Here's my share. But are you sure you love me?
MARION: I'm sure.
ROBIN: I'm glad you're not ashamed to say it.
MARION: And what's here?
ROBIN: A bagpipe I borrowed in the village. Isn't it beautiful?

[8] Hornplayers in the original.

THE PLAY OF ROBIN AND MARION 103

MARION: Sit next to me, love, and the others over there.
ROBIN: With all my heart.

(They all sit in a circle.)

MARION: Dinner is served! This piece is for you, dear. Simon! You're dreaming!
SIMON: I was thinking about Robin. If we hadn't happened to be cousins I would surely have fallen in love with you myself. What a body! Look, Walter.
ROBIN: Hands off! She's mine, not yours.
SIMON: What, jealous already?
ROBIN: Yes, by God.
MARION: Don't be afraid, Robin.
ROBIN: Can't I see that he's still pawing you?
MARION: Stay away, Simon. I don't like all this fooling. Let's think about our entertainment.
SIMON: I can sing lots of tales of chivalry.[9] Would you like to hear one?
ROBIN: Go ahead.
SIMON: Everybody listen. *(He sings.)*
　　Sir Lancelot set down his lance,
　　Foul was his cramp, down went his pants—
ROBIN: That's enough! I don't want to hear anymore! Aren't you ever going to change? You and your gutter ballads.
SIMON: You're a fool to be scolding me for my nice lyrics. Don't tell me it wasn't a good song.
ROBIN: It was not.
ALICE: I've got an idea. Let's dance a morris. Robin will lead, Harry will play on the bagpipe, and these two will fiddle.
MARION: We'll remove all the food. Robin, where's your hand now?
ROBIN: Oh I'm so unhappy. . . .

---

[9] I.e., *Chansons de geste*, chivalric lays or epics, of which the *Chanson de Roland* is a famous example. By the thirteenth century, parodies of tales of chivalry were already making the rounds (Chaucer's Sir Thopas is a latecomer, and Cervantes ends the tradition). Simon begins to sing the particularly obscene parody known as the tale of *Audigier*.

MARION: Silly. Come here and let me hug you.
ROBIN: That hug did wonders for me; you'll see me lead the morris like a master. But first I want you to dance with me to show how good we are together.
MARION: I'm willing. Here we go. But keep your hand where it belongs.

(Dance and music.)

MARION: God! That was a heavenly dance.
ROBIN: Do I know how to dance, Marion?
MARION: I should say so. It gives me the shivers when I see how you frisk about.
ROBIN: And now I'll lead the morris. Everybody up; hand in hand and follow me. Marion, give me your glove to keep, it will put fire into me.

(They dance to the music.)

ALICE: Ah, he's wonderful. Long live Robin!
ROBIN *(Singing.)*:
> Follow follow follow
> Up the hill and round the hollow,
> And till the sun falls down the tree,
> Follow follow follow me.

THE END

Peter Quill's Shenanigans
(LA FARCE DE MAÎTRE PIERRE PATHELIN)

Author Unknown

The farce of Pierre Pathelin (or Patelin) is the jewel of French comedy before Molière. Its hero has been a household name in France for five centuries. To this day the play has retained its vogue, and it is probably the only medieval play other than *Everyman* that is widely known, read, and performed beyond its own borders.

The first printed edition which has survived goes back to 1485 or 1486. Inasmuch as the verb "pateliner" appears in a legal document in 1469, and the name "Patelin" in an edifying poem that may have been written in the 1460's, it has been concluded that the farce was already popular twenty years before the 1485 edition appeared. Since, however, it is also possible that the author *used* rather than *created* the famous rogue, it cannot be decisively shown that 1465 is a better date for the play than 1485. Its subsequent popularity, however, is unquestionable. Five editions appeared before 1500, and over twenty were issued in the sixteenth century. The second half only of the play appeared as a prose anecdote without the name of Pathelin in an English book of "Merry Tales" in 1535. This suggests, incidentally, that the French playwright himself may have used a story already in circulation. It was through Rabelais, who loved and used the farce, that the true Pathelin crossed into England.

No one has successfully identified the author, though a plausible case has been made for a certain Guillaume Alexis, a Norman poet and priest. An even more plausible line of argument leaves the writer wrapped in his anonymity, but places him squarely in Paris as a barrister or a law student. Like the Templars of London in Shakespeare's time, the law students of fifteenth-century Paris were enthusiastic playgoers, producers, actors, and writers. Incorporated in a veritable little kingdom of their own, called the Basoche, the law clerks of Paris—there were some ten thousand of them—had acquired a virtual monopoly over the staging of comedies in the capital. It must be remembered that professional companies did not exist in the Europe of 1485. The Basochiens, who staged farces, moralities, and satiric revues called *sotties*, either for their own entertainment or for the general public, were all amateurs, though undoubtedly very gifted ones.

These law clerks were not necessarily humble scribblers in the offices of their betters. Many of them were graduates of law schools serving an apprenticeship of several years before becoming full-fledged advocates. Since they constituted a good portion of the intelligentsia of their time, it is not surprising if one of them—or perhaps an advocate who had been a Basochien in his youth—was able to toss off a farce as pungently sophisticated as that of Master Pathelin. Armed with a gift for graceful and rapid octosyllabic verse, the author of *Pathelin* took two quite separate stories, and stitched them together in the best Homeric manner, that is to say brilliantly if not faultlessly.

It used to be thought that the play deals with villagers and a small-town practitioner, but this view has been exploded in a recent study by a French scholar, Rita Lejeune. Not only was the play written for a metropolitan audience, but the action itself takes place in a big city, Paris itself according to Miss Lejeune. At first we are in the Latin Quarter where Pathelin lives. Then we move to the Right Bank, around the Halles, where the draper runs his shop. The shepherd is pasturing—and butchering—the cloth merchant's flock by the Seine, in grassland where the law students walked and played in their leisure hours. Since this land belonged to the abbey of Saint-Germain-des-Prés, the case of the peccant shepherd fell within the abbey's small autonomous jurisdiction.

Even if we do not accept this detailed localization of the action—which is, at any rate, useless for us today—it is important to visualize the action in a crowded city, for only thus can we explain the fact that Pathelin's exposure in the pillory (which I have translated as a few days in jail) is not known to the other characters, and does not prevent him from plying his trade.

Again without localizing the action, another scholar, Howard G. Harvey, has shown that the courtroom scene is by no means a generalized, simplified, "literary" creation, but, quite on the contrary, that it authentically represents the procedure of French lower courts, particularly the ecclesiastical ones. The informal proceedings, the direct questioning of both parties, and especially the intervention of an unlicensed pleader like Pathelin, were normal in these ecclesiastical courts, whether at Saint-Germain-des-Prés or in obscure villages. For the modern reader, however, the situation remains artificial. There is no rescuing it through learned notes. He has to accept the courtroom action as a farcical simplification of reality, though a meaningful one.

However this may be, Pathelin is clearly not a licensed attorney but a small-time pettifogger, a "clerc de taverne," possibly a tonsured rogue in minor orders working in a lowly capacity for the church and dispensing legal advice to anyone willing to treat him to a bottle of wine. This fixer is, however, on good terms with at least one judge, an honest one at that (as far as we know), and since even his wife admits that he once had a crowd of clients, we may have to allow his claim that he knows more about the law than many a rich and licensed barrister.

With *Pathelin* we come as close to comedy of character as we ever get on the medieval stage. True, this is still a farce concerning trickery. The situation is one that never fails to satisfy: the rascal who is outrascaled. And here the action is even more savory, for the rascal is outrascaled at his own advice. This is as artful as the situation that Machiavelli concocts in his *Mandragola*, where the cuckold himself keeps urging his wife to gratify him with a set of horns. But when all this is said, something else remains that the other farces and indeed the Italian comedies of the Renaissance do not have: a memorable character. We see Pathelin—our Peter Quill—at home, in the draper's shop, in court, with the shepherd—we know him poor but dishonest, sure of himself, gleeful and then mad as a hornet—and it is doubtful if we know Molière's miser any better.

The other characters are scarcely less alive. Whereas, for all their separate presences, the three rascals of Bodel's play belong to the same generic group, here we find a frisky courtroom parasite, a joyless, narrow-eyed merchant, and, a good social notch down, a clod who parlays openmouthed idiocy into genius: three discrete individuals in three different occupations. Add wife and judge, and the result is a minor triumph of human orchestration.

But characters are made memorable by what they do. And in *Pathelin* the intrigue, which the characters set in motion by virtue of what they are, never sags, never misses, never strays. It will not allow the spectator to turn his attention off for a moment. "How will he dupe the merchant?" "Will he get away with carrying the cloth home?" "What will he do when the merchant comes to claim his money?" Every episode answers a question and raises another. Besides, there is an especial pleasure in watching the strategy of three smart operators. When fools err, we may smile; but when the cunning stumble, we laugh out loud.

Like every good farce, this one has the authentic note of madness. The two main tricks—Quill's delirium and the shepherd's "baa"—are literally defiances of language, outrages against reason. Two reasonable designs—both of collecting money for services rendered, and what could be more reasonable?—are defeated by incoherence and imbecility, sound and fury. Still, this does not mean that we obtain a picture of an irrational world, for the irrationality is calculated in cold reason; it is intelligent strategy.

Intelligence is in the characters, and intelligence is in the execution of the plot. But we must be on our guard against deriving "visions of the world" from farce. Farce is a form of fantasy. It is a fantasy of absolute toughness linked to absolute harmlessness: a condition as clearly impossible in the real world as are coaches that turn into pumpkins at midnight. Farce throws off an air of reality because its people are utterly solid and everyday. But its world of inhumanity without suffering and brutality without injury (in which the mind finds deep conflicting desires reconciled) is in fairyland. It is ultimately because farce does *not* give us a picture of the world that we like it so much—and that we do not like it all the time.

Quill's trick upon Joss, and Tib's trick upon Quill, are far less real than the events in Bodel's tavern despite their jaunty realistic airs. Setting aside the miraculous appearance of Saint Nicholas, we have nothing in the activities of Bodel's tavern-keeper, waiter, town crier, and thieves that defies verisimilitude. No tricks are played in that tavern, and this is almost enough to tell us that Bodel has not written a farce but a "realistic comedy of low life." Genuine farce takes its brutalities into never-never land. In Bodel's play the thieves must hand over the goods in the end, for otherwise he would be writing an immoral play: a realistic play *can* be immoral. But in the farce justice is not done. Who cares? Fantasy is not moral or immoral, it is not dangerous.

What *Saint Nicolas* and *Pathelin* have in common is that neither relies on witty dialogue. No medieval play does. I do not know if there is any literature of witty repartee in the Middle Ages. Here is a question that calls for a collaboration between social and literary historians. Medieval literature is strong in the most elementary form of comedy, that of raw situation. It has wonderful examples of comedy of character, chiefly in Chaucer. But apparently certain refinements, possibly those involving ladies at court, were still lacking, and the witty banter of a Rosalind was an edge too fine, it would seem, for the Middle Ages to hone.

I have made a few cuts where the original is merely repetitious, and I have done my will with a very few passages where the French has yielded no satisfactory meaning even to the experts in this field. Where Quill raves in French, German, Spanish, and Italian, Pathelin jabbered in various French dialects, in Flemish, and in Latin—at greater length, I might add, than I have allowed him to do. Miss Lejeune must be right when she surmises that the fun here was addressed especially to the students who came from various parts of France and from what is now Belgium; perhaps, as she suggests, some of them helped the author patch these passages together. In keeping with the spirit of our times, I have not bowdlerized these and other speeches, but I have diminished them a little on the ground that even we, even today, are not able to take scatology so lightly as our ancestors did in 1485. I am justified, I think, in defying the fashion by reducing the coarseness of the original text just enough to preserve its joyous insouciance.

The staging of *Peter Quill* should present no difficulties. Peter's house is placed at one side of the stage and the draper's shop at the other. The courtroom can be mounted in the center rear. The space between will then be the street. To indicate greater distances and longer intervals, the characters can walk off-stage before they reappear, instead of making straight for one of the sites on stage.

For my translation I have again used Pauphilet's *Jeux et Sapience du Moyen Âge*. I have also consulted the notes in Barbara C. Bowen's edition of the play in her *Four Farces* (Oxford: Blackwell's French Texts, 1967), and such material as is available in specialized articles.

BIBLIOGRAPHY

HOLBROOK, RICHARD T. *Master Pierre Patelin.* Boston, 1914. Holbrook's introduction gives the basic facts.

FRANK, GRACE. *The Medieval French Drama.* Oxford, 1954. Chapter XXIV deals with comedy in the fifteenth and sixteenth centuries.

HARVEY, HOWARD G. *The Theatre of the Basoche.* Cambridge, 1941.

PETER QUILL'S SHENANIGANS

CHARACTERS

Peter Quill
Madge, his wife
Joss, a cloth merchant
Tib, a shepherd
Judge

PETER QUILL'S *house.*

PETER: God help me, Madge, I wear myself out scraping and scrounging, and still we can't make ends meet. Where are the days when I was turning the clients away?
MADGE: I was just thinking about this lawyering of yours myself. Time was when everybody in town was flocking to you to consult you about their disputes. Now they call you Mr. Flop.
PETER: And yet—I don't mean to boast—there isn't a better legal brain in the city than mine, except for the judge's.
MADGE: Well, he's got schooling. He even has a degree.
PETER: So what? I'm no bookworm, but I can fix just about any case I put my hand to. I can talk better than a priest can sing.
MADGE: That's a blessing! We can't afford a pair of shoes, we're starving to death, and our garments are worn through to their linings. How is your legal brain going to help us to some new clothes?
PETER: Down, woman. If the spirit moves me, I'll get you all the dresses, hoods, and hats you want. Patience. Before long, the good Lord will pull us out of this hole. Yes, by

PETER QUILL'S SHENANIGANS 113

God! You'll see wonders once I decide to put my talent to work.

MADGE: Wonders of skullduggery. I know. Nobody can say you're behindhand when it comes to a crooked deal.

PETER: I'm talking about the legal profession, woman, exercised with dignity.

MADGE: And I'm talking about picking pockets, your specialty. Even though you're an illiterate clown, you've got a reputation for being able to argue the hangman out of his rope.

PETER: True, the art of pleading holds no secrets for me.

MADGE: The art of cheating is what you mean. Anyway, that's what people say about you.

PETER: That's what they say about a lot of phony lawyers who know a great deal less than I do; in spite of which they've got twenty suits hanging in their closets. Well, we've chattered enough. I'm going marketing.

MADGE: Marketing?

PETER: Yes, marketing, my love. I hope you won't mind if I look for a bit of material or some knickknacks we need in the household. Our clothes *are* getting threadbare, there's no denying it.

MADGE: You haven't got a penny and you know it. What are you dreaming up?

PETER: Wouldn't you like to know, my beauty? But never trust me again if I don't come home with enough cloth to fit both of us out. What color do you like best? Gray? Green? Do you favor tweed? Herringbone? Don't be shy.

MADGE: Anything will do. Beggars can't be choosers.

PETER: Two-and-a-half yards for you, and three for me, why not four? Altogether—

MADGE: I'm glad you're not skimping, but who the dickens is going to give you credit?

PETER: Leave it to me. I'll get a loan, don't worry, and repay it on doomsday at the earliest.

MADGE: Well, that's more like it. Go ahead, love, let's see who gets stuck with it.

PETER: I'll buy either gray or green, plus some brown material

for a lining, let me see, three-quarters of a yard or a full yard.
MADGE: Listen to the man! On your way! And if you run into King Solomon, I don't mind if he stands you a drink.
PETER: Take care of the house. *(Exit.)*
MADGE: Who's the merchant he's going to diddle? I hope he gets away with it.

JOSS's *shop*.

PETER: Is this the place? Yes it is, and there's my man. Good day, and God be with you.
JOSS: Good day, and God's peace to you.
PETER: What a treat! I haven't seen you in ages, Mr. Joss. How have you been? In good health and chipper?
JOSS: Oh yes.
PETER: Let me shake your hand.
JOSS: And how are you, Mr. Quill?
PETER: Happy to see you in good spirits.
JOSS: Oh well—you know the retail trade; life is no bed of roses for us.
PETER: How is business, though? You're doing well, I hope.
JOSS: I don't know. So-so. Mostly it's hard work.
PETER: As I look at you, my mind goes back to your father, may he rest in peace. Such a brain! Such a business head! You're as like to him as one pea is to another. I could swear it's him I was talking to. May God have mercy on his soul.
JOSS: Amen, and on ours too.
PETER: He had a way of seeing the future that was uncanny. I've never forgotten it. And what a sweet disposition!
JOSS: Sit down, won't you? I should have asked you before. It's my way. . . .
PETER: I don't mind standing. God, when I remember him—
JOSS: Sit down, sit down!
PETER: Certainly. *(He sits.)* "Wait and see," he'd say, "just wait and see; there will be extraordinary developments!" Same ears, same nose, same mouth, same eyes. Even the cleft in the chin! Anybody who'd tell your mother that you're not

your father's child would be asking for a first-rate libel suit. Seriously, I don't understand how Nature could ever make two faces so exactly alike, even the pimples. If I spat twice against the wall, the likeness wouldn't be more than between you and your dad. By the way, what about Mrs. Lawrence, your beautiful aunt, didn't she pass away?

JOSS: Of course not!

PETER: What a gorgeous creature she was! Tall, straight, graceful. You've inherited her shape, you know. As like as two snowmen! I guess there's not another family in town for these fantastic resemblances. The more I see you—there!—it's your father standing before me! What a fine man he was! And whoever needed merchandise on credit—"Take it, take it" he'd say, no questions asked. Lovely man! God have mercy on his soul. The times we had together! Joking and laughing, him and me! If only the rest of the world resembled him, we wouldn't be robbing each other blind night and day. *(He rises and feels a piece of cloth.)* Say, this is fine material! Beautiful, soft, and smooth.

JOSS: I have it made specially from the wool of my own sheep.

PETER: You know how to run your shop and no mistake. Otherwise you wouldn't be your father's son. Always busy, never a moment's rest.

JOSS: What do you expect? A man earns his living by the sweat of his brow.

PETER *(Feeling another piece of goods.)*: Is this one dyed before it's woven? It feels as solid as a piece of Spanish leather.

JOSS: It's a local cloth, of very fine quality indeed.

PETER: I'm really tempted. God knows I wasn't intending to buy anything when I came in. I'd set a hundred and twenty dollars aside to pay off a loan, but I can see that a good chunk of it is going to be yours. The color is so beautiful I can't resist it. I'll want some for myself and some for my wife.

JOSS: It's an expensive material, I'd better warn you.

PETER: I don't care. Quality is what counts. Besides, between you and me, I've got a little something under the mattress, mum's the word.

JOSS: Very nice; I'm all for that.
PETER: In short, I'm crazy about this cloth and I must have a piece of it.
JOSS: How many yards would you like? It's all at your disposal, and I wish I could give it away free.
PETER: I know, and I thank you with all my heart.
JOSS: Would you like it in blue?
PETER: What does it cost? Wait—before we go on, I want to put something in your almsbox. Here's my penny for the orphans.
JOSS: You're a man of charity, Mr. Quill. Shall I quote you my bottom price?
PETER: Please do.
JOSS: This will cost you six-and-a-half dollars a yard.
PETER: Six-and-a-half dollars a yard? Out of the question.
JOSS: I swear to God, that's what I paid for it myself, I can't go any lower.
PETER: Too much.
JOSS: You don't realize how prices have gone up. Why, think of the livestock that froze to death last winter!
PETER: Five-fifty.
JOSS: Impossible. I'm paying double the old price for my wool this year, the scarcity is terrific.
PETER: Well, if that's how it is, I won't haggle with you. Go ahead and measure.
JOSS: How many yards?
PETER: Three for me, two and a half for Madge—she's a big girl, you know. Altogether six yards. Wait—I'm stupid!
JOSS: Add another half and you'll have an even six yards.
PETER: All right, just to round off the figure. Besides, I need a cape.
JOSS: Hold this end; we'll measure it off together without scrimping. One, two, three, four, five, six.
PETER: On the nose.
JOSS: I'll be glad to measure again.
PETER: Oh no. A little more, a little less, it's all the same to me. How much do I owe you now?

PETER QUILL'S SHENANIGANS

JOSS: We'll figure it out. At six-fifty a yard, six yards will come to thirty-nine dollars.

PETER: Very good. I'll pay you in full if you'll step over to my house in an hour.

JOSS: I don't know. It's a long detour for me.

PETER: Well spoken, Mr. Joss, every word that falls from your lips is pure gospel. That's exactly what you'll do—make a detour to my house. You've never paid us a call, but this time you will, and we'll have a drink together.

JOSS: I drink enough as it is. Every time I make a sale I have to clinch it over a drink. I'll do it, Mr. Quill, but I don't like to give credit to a new customer.

PETER: How would you like it if I paid you in gold? And not only that. I want you to stay for dinner. We're having a roast duck tonight.

JOSS: You're a hard man to put off, Mr. Quill. All right—it's a deal—I'll stop by your house with the cloth.

PETER: I wouldn't dream of it! I'll carry it under my arm, it won't bother me one bit.

JOSS: Oh no, it'll be an inconvenience to you. I'll carry it.

PETER: Absolutely not. I'm not going to let you get out of breath for my sake. Let me take it. Snug under my arm. See? No trouble at all. And don't forget we'll have a blast at my house!

JOSS: You'll pay me as soon as I arrive?

PETER: You bet. No! Come to think of it, not before you've sunk your teeth into that duckling. I almost wish I didn't have the cash, so I'd see you more often at my place and we could crack a few bottles together. Oh your late father—never walked past our house without poking his head inside. "Anybody home?" or "What's the good word today?" or "How's my old chum?" But you capitalists, of course, you don't care for those of us that haven't made it big.

JOSS: Who's a capitalist? I'm practically a pauper.

PETER: Ha, ha, tell me more! Well, I'm off. Come soon, and bring your thirst along.

JOSS: Fine, fine. I'll be along, and don't forget you're paying me in gold.

PETER: Don't be anxious. I've never let anybody down. *(In the street.)* Gold is it? I'll see him hanged first. He stuck to his price, but he'll be paid at mine. We'll see about gold. I'd like to have him jogging till he was paid in full, he'd be running from here to the South Pole. *(Exit.)*

JOSS: I'll keep the gold snug in my sock for a year so it won't catch cold. The moral of the story is, it takes a fox to catch a fox. Though come to think of it, this particular fox was an ass, he paid six-and-a-half dollars for my cloth when five would have been too much!

QUILL's *house.*

PETER *(Entering.)*: What have I got under my arm?

MADGE: Well, what?

PETER: Say, whatever happened to your Sunday dress?

MADGE: You know perfectly well what happened to it. What do you want to do with it?

PETER: Nothing, nothing. Because—what do you think I've brought home? Is this what you wanted?

MADGE: God have mercy on us! The man's become a highway robber! Oh lord! There's going to be trouble. Who'll pay for this?

PETER: It's all paid, my beauty. The draper who sold it to me is no fool, but all the same I'll be damned if I didn't bleed that sourpuss as white as a sack of plaster.

MADGE: How much did it cost?

PETER: Nothing, I tell you. It's paid, do you hear, paid.

MADGE: Paid? How? You didn't have a copper penny in your pocket.

PETER: That's a lie. I did have a penny on me.

MADGE: I understand: you signed a note, and when it falls due, they'll carry every stick of furniture out of the house.

PETER: Nothing of the kind. This cloth, I'm telling you, cost me a total of one penny.

MADGE: Mary mother of God. You're raving.

PETER: If he saw, or ever will see, more than the penny I spent, I'll give you my right eye to pluck out.

MADGE: Who was it?
PETER: Bill Joss, if you must know.
MADGE: Explain about the penny. How did you do it?
PETER: I put a penny in his almsbox. And as for that, if I hadn't wanted to, I needn't have put it in. But I'm satisfied. Let him split the penny with the good Lord, because that's all they'll wring out of me, I don't care if they sing, dance, or holler for more.
MADGE: How did you get that skinflint to trust you?
PETER: I blabbed so much about his wonderful family, I thought he was going to make me a present of the cloth. You should have heard me carry on about his father. "Mr. Joss," I said to him, "the best blood of the county flows in your veins." God forgive me, I remember his dad, that stubborn shaggy runt. "My good friend," says I, "you bear a perfect resemblance to your father." And then more jabber, and after that compliments for his merchandise. "Furthermore," I said, "he was always willing to give credit to his customers with a smile on his lips. Yes, the resemblance between you is amazing!" The fact of the matter is, it would have been easier to pull teeth out of Joss senior and Joss junior, the brutes, than squeeze credit or a good word out of them. But I rattled on till he did give me the whole six yards on credit.
MADGE: And you'll never pay him?
PETER: Pay him? I'll let the devil pay him.
MADGE: This is like the story about the crow who was sitting on a branch high in a tree with a piece of cheese in his bill. Along comes a fox, and first thing, he sees the cheese. So he sits down at the foot of the tree and calls out to the crow. "My oh my," he says, "but you're a handsome bird, and what a sweet voice you've got." The silly crow gets all worked up when he hears his singing praised, so he opens his beak to show off his voice, the cheese falls to the ground, the fox grabs it and he's off like a shot. And that's the way you bamboozled Joss out of his cloth.
PETER: Which reminds me, I invited him to dine off a roast duck with us. Listen carefully. He'll be here any moment

yelling for his cash. I'll lie down and play sick. As soon as he opens his mouth, you tell him, "Hush, keep your voice down." Then you give a loud groan and look as miserable as you can. "Lord have mercy," you'll say, "he's been sick for two months or six weeks." And if he answers, "Fiddle-faddle, the man left my shop an hour ago," you'll moan, "Oh Lord, is this a time for jokes?" Let me take care of the rest. I intend to pipe him a tune he'll never forget.

MADGE: Trust me to play my part, but if you run foul of the law again, you'll be in twice the hot water you were in after your last scrape.

PETER: Peace in the house! I know what I'm about. Do as I tell you.

MADGE: Don't forget the Saturday you spent in the lockup and a mob almost lynched you.

PETER: Stop reminiscing. We're forgetting it's getting late and Joss'll be here any minute. I'm going to lie down in bed.

MADGE: Go ahead.

PETER: And don't burst out laughing.

MADGE: Don't worry. I'll cry my heart out.

JOSS's *shop.*

JOSS: Time to close shop. Shall I pour myself the usual before going home? No. I'm supposed to have a drink at Quill's house, not to mention the roast duck and my money. At the very least I'll get a free snack. Might as well go now, I don't expect any more customers.

QUILL's *house.*

JOSS: Anybody home? Mr. Quill!

MADGE *(Letting him in.)*: Silence, for heaven's sake! If you have anything to say, say it softly.

JOSS: Good afternoon, Mrs. Quill.

MADGE: Softer!

JOSS: What's that?

MADGE: I'm telling you—
JOSS: Where is he?
MADGE: Oh God, where should he be?
JOSS: Where should who be?
MADGE: It isn't kind of you to ask, dear Mr. Joss. The poor wretch is where he's been these eleven weeks without stirring.
JOSS: Who are you—
MADGE: Excuse me if I don't talk any louder. I think he's resting a bit. Oh Jesus, you should see how low he is!
JOSS: Who?
MADGE: My husband, Peter.
JOSS: Who are you talking about? Didn't he pick up six yards of cloth in my store just now?
MADGE: Who? Peter?
JOSS: Two hours ago! One hour ago! Don't keep me standing here; I haven't got all day. Stop this fiddle-faddle and give me my money.
MADGE: This is no time for joking, Mr. Joss.
JOSS: My money! Have you gone mad? My thirty-nine dollars!
MADGE: Mr. Joss, you're not in a lunatic asylum. Why don't you go and entertain your cronies instead of pestering me?
JOSS: I'll curse God if I don't get my thirty-nine dollars!
MADGE: I'm sorry, but we don't all feel like fooling around.
JOSS: Mrs. Quill, stop this nonsense and call Mr. Quill.
MADGE: Is this going to go on all day?
JOSS: Am I or am I not in Mr. Quill's house?
MADGE: I hope you drop dead if you don't lower your voice!
JOSS: What's that? Can't I even ask for him?
MADGE: Quiet, you'll wake him.
JOSS: What is it you want? Am I supposed to whisper in your ear or talk from the cellar or from the bottom of a well?
MADGE: I guess God made you a loudmouth and there's no help for it.
JOSS: Devils in hell! All right, I'll keep my voice down. I'm not used to this kind of squabbling. All right. Mr. Quill made off today with six yards of my cloth.
MADGE: What? What's that? Made off, made off? I hope they

hang the liar that said it! Oh my poor husband! Eleven weeks in a coma and I have to listen to this slop! Clear out of here, stop tormenting a helpless woman!

JOSS: You told me to keep my voice down. Who's shouting now?

MADGE: You're looking for a fight, aren't you?

JOSS: Well, if you want me to leave the house, hand me—

MADGE: Softer!

JOSS: You're the one who'll wake him up! Your voice is ten times louder than mine. Come on, Mrs. Quill, don't keep me waiting any longer.

MADGE: I see it now: you're drunk.

JOSS: Drunk? Me? God punish you!

MADGE: Not so loud!

JOSS: Madam, I demand, for six yards of cloth—

MADGE: The cloth again! Who did you give it to?

JOSS: To *him*!

MADGE: Is he fit for a piece of cloth? He can't even lift an arm. The only cloth he'll ever see will be white, and it'll be wrapped around him when he leaves this house feet first.

JOSS: All this must have just happened, because I talked to him today.

MADGE: Down with your voice!

JOSS: It's you, devils in hell, you, blood and damnation! Pay me and I'll go! *(Aside.)* This is what happens every time I'm fool enough to give credit.

PETER *(From his curtained four-poster.)*: Madge! The smelling salts. Prop me up a bit. . . . Put a pillow under me. . . . Water! Who am I talking to? Somebody please rub the soles of my feet.

JOSS: That's his voice.

MADGE: Sure.

PETER: Come here, you trollop. Didn't I tell you to open the windows? Cover me up. Drive these black people away!
                Marmara!
                Carimara!
                Carimara!

MADGE: What's the matter? Look at the way you're tossing about! Are you crazy?
PETER: You can't see what I see! There's a witch flying in the room! Catch her! There's a black cat! Look at it going up!
MADGE: Stop tossing! Aren't you ashamed of yourself?
PETER: These doctors are killing me with their drugs. And a man can't argue with them. We're all putty in their hands.
MADGE: Poor man! *(To* JOSS.*)* Go on, take a look at him, see how sick he is.
JOSS: Did he really become ill after returning from my shop?
MADGE: Your shop?
JOSS: Yes, that's where he was, I think. The cloth I lent you, Mr. Quill, I have to have the money for it.
PETER: Oh doctor, today in my stool there were two small pellets, each one black and round and hard as a stone. Should I take another enema?
JOSS: How do I know? I want my thirty-nine dollars.
PETER: What about these three sharp objects you gave me, doctor, do you call those pills? They nearly broke my jaws. Don't make me take them anymore, for pity's sake. They were so bitter I threw them up.
JOSS: Why don't you throw up my thirty-nine dollars?
MADGE: People like you should be strung up! Get out of here!
JOSS: Not before I get my cloth or my money.
PETER: And what about my urine? Does it look fatal? Dear God, don't let me die, no matter how long I have to suffer!
MADGE *(To* JOSS.*):* Go away! You should be ashamed to be making him delirious.
JOSS: Am I supposed to forget about my six yards of cloth? You tell me—is that fair?
PETER: Couldn't you take a look at my feces, doctor? They're so hard, I don't know how I'm surviving, it hurts so much when I push.
JOSS: I want my money!
MADGE: Oh Jesus, how can you go on tormenting the poor man? Can't you see he's mistaken you for the doctor? Eleven weeks in bed, poor Christian, without a break.

JOSS: But how could this have happened to him? He came to see me today and we made a deal, or so I thought, I don't know what's what anymore.
MADGE: Your mind is a little shaky, Mr. Joss. Take my advice, really, go home and lie down. People might think that you came here for my sake. And the doctors will be here in a minute.
JOSS: I don't care what dirty people think as long as I'm not thinking any dirt. *(Aside.)* Damnation, has it come to that? *(To* MADGE.*)* Look here, I thought—
MADGE: Still at it?
JOSS: Aren't you roasting a duck?
MADGE: What a question! Roast duck for a sick man? Go on, eat your own ducks and don't come here with your blabber. Can't you see you're intruding?
JOSS: I don't mean to offend you, but it was my impression—
MADGE: Again?
JOSS: God damn you both and good-bye! *(He goes outside.)* Devils in hell, I know he took six yards all in one piece, but this woman has managed to muddle my brain. I know he took them. No he didn't. It doesn't make sense. I saw him in the grip of death. Or was he faking? Damn it, he did take six yards, he stuck the bolt under his arm, I saw it. Or did I? Maybe I'm dreaming. Since when do I give my goods away on credit? Which means he hasn't got the cloth. Yes he has. No he hasn't. Has. Hasn't. I'm going mad. I don't know who's right. It's a bottomless pit. *(Exit.)*
PETER: Is he gone?
MADGE: Be still; I'm listening. He's going off mumbling and grumbling God knows what.
PETER: I might as well get out of bed.
MADGE: No, don't! He could be back any moment, and if he finds you up we'll both be hanged.
PETER: Oh Jesus, how we baited that suspicious dunderhead! A dunce cap on Bill Joss would look better than a crucifix in church.
MADGE: And serves him right—a pennypincher who leaves a

shirt button in the collection plate on Sundays. Oh Lord oh Lord!
PETER: Hush, don't laugh, for God's sake. I'm sure he's coming back.
MADGE: I can't stop.

JOSS *(In his shop.)*: Yes, by the holy shining sun, I'm going back to that shyster's house whether he likes it or not. I know his kind—he'd put his own mother behind bars for an IOU. The rascal has my cloth, I gave it to him here, on this very spot.

MADGE: When I think of the face he made when he looked at you, oh I've got to laugh! Give me my money! Six yards!
PETER: Stop laughing, I tell you. If he comes back and hears you, that's it; we'll have to beat it out of town.

JOSS *(In the street.)*: That courthouse parasite, does he think we're all cretins? I'll have him strung up on a tree. He's got my cloth and he's trying to skin me. God strike me dead if he isn't. *(He returns to* QUILL'*s house.)* Laughter! Open the door!
MADGE *(Low.)*: Oh God, he heard me!
PETER *(Low.)*: I'll pretend I'm delirious. Go on.
MADGE *(Opening the door.)*: What's all the shouting about?
JOSS: So you're laughing, are you? Good enough. Hand over my money.
MADGE: Merciful heavens, I was laughing? At what? I'm in agony. He's sinking fast. You never heard such a storm and frenzy. He's raving, singing, and jabbering away in a dozen languages—he'll be gone in half an hour, and that's why I'm laughing and crying all at the same time.
JOSS: I don't know about laughing and crying, but, to make a long story short, I want my money.
MADGE: Are we starting all over again?
JOSS: I'm a businessman, I'm used to straightforward talk. Do you think I can't tell a bull from a cow?

PETER: Up, Madge, up! It's the Queen of Mandolina! Let her come in! I know she's been delivered of twenty-four tiny Mandolinnies, the bishop is their daddy and I'm requested to be the godfather.
MADGE: Alas, alas, set your mind on God the Father, my dear Peter, and not on Mandolinnies.
JOSS: What in hell does this drivel mean? Money! I want my money!
MADGE: Stop harassing my poor husband! But when I look at your face I realize you're insane. If only I had somebody to help, I'd have you tied up, you're a raving lunatic.
JOSS: I take a solemn oath that if I ever give credit again, I'll renounce God and deliver my soul to the devil.
PETER: Mon Dieu! Holy Virgin! Take me to la mer! Je suis tu suis il suis! Ding dong, frère Jacques, ding dong, ring ze bell mam'selle, but don't talk about ze money! *(To* JOSS.*)* Get it, brother?
MADGE: That was mostly French. One of his uncles, actually the brother of his uncle's wife, was a Frenchman.
JOSS: Nevertheless, he finagled me out of my cloth.
PETER: Herein, bitte, schöne Damen! Wer sind diese ugly toads? Teufelsdreck, heraus! Mach schnell, ich will bekommen ein priest! Why is the priest laughing, der Hund, mach ihm singen his Mass!
MADGE: Oh God have mercy on his soul, the time for the last sacrament is at hand.
JOSS: Wasn't that German he was talking just now?
MADGE: His mother was German, that's why?
PETER: Pépé, olé! I entiendo you, madre de Dios, it's good to see you as hermoso as ever, José! Let me pour you a leetle glass of tequila, no agua in it, no? Cheers! Bottoms up! Qué tal? Oh I want to confess!
JOSS: How many languages does he speak? If he'd only give me a small installment on his debt, I'd gladly leave.
MADGE: How can you be so stubborn? Oh I'm so unhappy!
PETER: Why dontcha talka to me, Giuseppe? My povero stomacco, ai ai ai, she hurta so much, she busta my culo, oh

sole mio, pasta asciutta! Belle signorine, catcha this fly before she stinga me, per favore!
JOSS: Where does he find the strength to talk so much? (QUILL *does a death rattle.*) He's going mad!
MADGE: It's the end. His schoolteacher came from Italy, and now with his last breath he remembers him.
JOSS: This is the strangest day of my life. I could have sworn he was in my store today, but I guess I was mistaken.
PETER: Et bona dies sit vobis, magister amantissime, pater reverendissime.
MADGE: Latin! He's really dying. His last words show his veneration for God. And I'm going to be left a widow without a penny.
JOSS (*Aside.*): I'd better get out of here. (*To* MADGE.) Your husband may have a few secrets to impart to you before he gives up the ghost, so I'll be going. Please forgive me. I really thought he had my cloth. Forgive me in God's name.
MADGE: A poor afflicted widow blesses you.
JOSS (*Aside.*): What a day! The devil must have disguised himself as Mr. Quill and stolen my cloth in order to lead me into temptation. Let him keep it and leave me in peace.

(*Exit.*)

PETER (*Jumping out of bed.*): I did it! And away he goes, handsome Joss, his mind in a whirl, and tonight the nightmares will gripe him!
MADGE: God, how we fuddled him! Didn't I perform like a star?
PETER: You did, my pigeon, and I'm proud of you. Where's the cloth? Look at it, enough for two new wardrobes!

The street.

JOSS: Everybody lies to me, everybody robs me. I'm the king of losers. Even the shepherds are swindling me, and God knows they're dumb. Just look at my man Tibbald trying to fleece me, though I've always been a good master to him. But he'll regret it, by God.

(*Enter* TIB.)

TIB: Good evening, sweet master. I hope God has granted you a happy day.

JOSS: It's you is it, you lousy yokel!

TIB: Excuse me for crossing your path, sir, but a man in a funny uniform came up to me, sir, he was all steamed up about I couldn't figure out what it was, it sounded sort of like Greek to me, but he was carrying on about you, and about summonses, and about sheep, and this report here and that report there, I got all confused.

JOSS: We'll see how confused you get when I drag you before the judge. Devils in hell! May tempests and floods drown me if you ever bludgeon another beast of mine! You'll make restitution to me, do you hear, my six yards, I mean my sheep, and the plunder you've had all ten years you've been working for me.

TIB: Don't believe in wicked gossip, my dearest master, because I swear to God—

JOSS: That before the week is out you'll return my cloth, I mean my sheep.

TIB: What cloth? Looks like you're upset about something else. Oh Lord, oh Lord, I'm so scared when I look at you I'm afraid to open my mouth.

JOSS: Get out of here, and you'll obey that summons if you know what's good for you.

TIB: Can't we settle out of court, sir? I'd as soon not meddle with the law.

JOSS: Get out I said. No settlement, no agreement, no compromise. Let the judge decide. Devils in hell, if I don't crack down right now, I'll be swindled at every streetcorner. (*He enters his shop.*)

TIB: God prosper you, sir. (*Alone.*) I'd better find somebody to defend me.

Before QUILL's *house.*

(TIB *knocks at the door.*)

TIB: Anyone home?
PETER: Damnation, he's come back again!
MADGE: If it's Joss, we're cooked!
TIB: It's me, Tibbald the shepherd.
PETER *(Stepping out.)*: God bless you, lad. Tell me what's on your mind.
TIB: Well, I'm going to be put in jail if I don't show up for a summons. You'll help me, won't you Mr. Quill? I want you to defend me, because I'm an ignoramus. And I'll pay you good money, don't let the rags I'm wearing fool you.
PETER: Very well, let's hear the matter. Are you the plaintiff or the defendant?
TIB: I'm the victim of a smart operator, sir, whose sheep I've been looking after for years. Well, as he didn't hardly pay me anything—should I tell you the whole story?
PETER: Sure. I'm your counsel; you mustn't hold anything back from me.
TIB: Well, the truth is, I gave some of them a knock between the ears, and would you believe it, they fainted away and then dropped dead, even the healthy ones. But I'd let on like they'd died of the scab, just so's I wouldn't get blamed. "Come on," says my employer, "better get rid of the animal so it won't contaminate the others." "Right," says I. But being that I knew what the disease really was, I carved 'em all up for my table. That's about all there is. I went on bashing 'em over the head and butchering 'em till he finally smelled the rat. He snuck after me, it was easy, you see, because when you hit 'em they bawl. And now he's caught me red-handed, I can't deny the fact. But I thought to myself, I thought maybe the two of us could trip him up somehow. I've got enough money for your fee, don't worry about that. Sure I know he's got the law on his side, but if

you set your mind to it you can find the articles and clauses that'll put him in the wrong.

PETER: What will you give me if I get you acquitted? Exactly how happy will you be?

TIB: Enough to give you solid gold, not paper money.

PETER: Consider the case won, even if it stinks to high heaven. The sounder my opponent's suit, the faster I demolish it once I decide to give it my best. Wait till you hear me smother him in objections. Come here. You're shrewd enough to understand a trick, I'm sure. Tell me first, what's your name?

TIB: Tibbald Woolly.

PETER: You've done your master out of how many sheep, my good Woolly?

TIB: Lemme see. More'n thirty in three years. They all tasted good.

PETER: That's ten a year, not bad for a second income. *(Aside.)* I'll milk him for all he's worth. *(To* TIB.*)* What about witnesses for the prosecution? Will he produce any? That's a capital point.

TIB: He'll find ten witnesses to swear against me before you got time to sneeze.

PETER: That's a serious handicap. Let me think. I'll pretend I haven't got anything to do with you. I'll just offer my advice as a friend of the court. In fact, I don't know you.

TIB: Hey, that's no good.

PETER: Don't worry. Next point. As soon as you say a word, they'll knock you over with a volley of facts and force you to confess. Nothing harms a case like a confession. So from the moment you're told to take the stand you'll say nothing except "Baa," whatever happens. Suppose they yell at you, "You dirty clod, do you think you can defy Justice, you miserable cur?" Just answer "Baa." "Oh dear," I'll put in, "he's feebleminded, he thinks he's talking to his flock." Let them burst their gut if they want to. You just keep answering "Baa," and nothing else. Do you think you can do it?

TIB: You bet! It's my interest, ain't it? You'll be proud of me.

PETER: Fine. And don't forget. "Baa" to everybody, even to me, no matter what I say or suggest.
TIB: You can count on me. From now on, come hell or high water, it's "Baa" for you and everybody, exactly like you taught me.
PETER: So much for your accuser. But don't forget to make it worth my while when we're finished.
TIB: Never trust me again if I don't pay you at your own word. But you'll do your best, won't you?
PETER: I will. Very good, Mr. Woolly, I'll see you in court. We'd better take separate ways.
TIB: Good idea, so nobody can tell you're my lawyer.
PETER: Remember now—I expect a generous fee.
TIB: Your word is my law, Mr. Quill. *(Exit.)*
PETER: Not bad, not bad. I won't get the crown jewels for this case, but every tidbit helps. It's small fry; but it's fish.

The courtroom.

PETER: My respectful greetings, your honor.
JUDGE: Welcome in court, Mr. Quill. Take a seat in front.

(Enter JOSS.*)*

PETER: Oops! I'd rather stay back here, thank you.
JUDGE: Next case. And let's hurry so we can adjourn for the day.
JOSS: My counsel will be here any moment, your honor. He's finishing work on another case. I hope you don't mind waiting a bit.
JUDGE: I certainly do mind. I have a hearing at the other end of town. Aren't you the plaintiff?
JOSS: Yes.
JUDGE: Where's the defendant?
JOSS: There he is. He's keeping his mouth shut, but he knows why he's here.
JUDGE: Since you're both present, let me hear your complaint.
JOSS: Here it is. For the love of God and for charity's sake I

raised this fellow when he was a child. When he was old enough to work I sent him to the fields to tend my livestock, and, in short, I made him my shepherd. But as true as you're sitting in front of me, your honor, he slaughtered so many of my lambs and sheep—

JUDGE: Wait a minute. Was the man under contract with you?

PETER: There we are! Because if he wasn't—

JOSS: You! God strike me dead if it isn't you!

JUDGE: Why are you holding your hand to your face, Mr. Quill? Have you got a toothache?[1]

PETER: Yes, one of my teeth is killing me. But don't let me interrupt you, your honor.

JUDGE: Continue, Mr. Joss, hurry up and speak clearly.

JOSS: He's the man, as I hope to live. I swear by the Cross on which Jesus was crucified, you're the man I sold six yards of cloth to, Mr. Quill!

JUDGE (To PETER.): What does he mean with his cloth?

PETER: His mind must be wandering. I imagine he's trying to state his argument, but he doesn't know how to go about it.

JOSS (To the JUDGE.): Blood and damnation! He's the one who took my cloth!

PETER: Not a bad schemer, I must say! Won't stop at anything to buttress his case. I know what he's insinuating—that the shepherd sold him the wool out of which my suit was made. In other words, the shepherd stole the wool off his sheep.

JOSS: You've got my cloth, by every saint in heaven!

JUDGE: Peace! Get back to your deposition and don't waste the court's time with cock-and-bull stories.

PETER: I can't help laughing even though my tooth hurts. Our plaintiff has forgotten where he left off. I think we'd better come to his rescue.

JUDGE: Well then, back to our sheep. What happened to them?

JOSS: He took six full yards, a thirty-nine dollar value.

JUDGE: Are you trying to make a jackass out of me? Where do you think you are?

---

[1] Quill is trying to play his part in Tib's defense and at the same time conceal himself from Joss, whom he had not expected to meet in court. The Judge's naming him puts a quick end to this ploy.

PETER: Tut tut. He's treating you as if *he* were the master here. Look at his shifty eyes. But, if I may, I'd like to advise that the defendant be questioned.
JUDGE: Good idea. *(To* TIB.*)* You, step forward. What do you say?
TIB: Baa.
JUDGE: Another headache! What does Baa mean? Am I a goat? Address yourself to me.
TIB: Baa.
JUDGE: God blast you! Are you mocking the bench?
PETER: I'd say he was loony or half-witted. He thinks he's grazing his flock.
JOSS: Strike me dead if it wasn't you—you—nobody else—that stole my cloth! Your honor, your honor, you don't know what a thief—
JUDGE: Silence! Are you going berserk? Drop the accessory details and let's get to the main point.
JOSS: I will, your honor, but this business is close to my heart. However, I swear I won't breathe another word about it today. Another time I will. Today I'll swallow my anger. As I was saying, I'd handed over six yards—I should say my sheep. Excuse me. My shepherd was supposed to be in the field—but he said I'd have my thirty-nine dollars as soon as I came—I mean—three years ago he swore to take loyal care of my flocks—he wouldn't rob me—he'd see no harm would come to my sheep—and then—and now—he denies everything—cloth, money, and all. Yes, you do, Mr. Quill! I mean—the scoundrel was shearing my beasts on the sly, and cudgeling the best of them to death. Then, with my six yards of cloth under his arm, he ran off and told me to collect at his house.
JUDGE: There's no rhyme or reason in your testimony. Now it's this and now it's that. I'm swamped in cloth and sheep, and I've yet to hear a sentence with a beginning and an end.
PETER: I'm sure he starves his poor shepherd besides.
JOSS: Shut up, you! My cloth! Don't I know better than anybody where the shoe pinches? You have it!
JUDGE: What does he have?

JOSS: Nothing, your honor. But I swear he's the worst conniver —enough, my lips are sealed, I won't mention it again.

JUDGE: Why don't you try to remember the facts and come to a clear conclusion?

PETER: I don't see how that poor shepherd can answer the charges without legal counsel, and either he doesn't know how or he doesn't dare ask for it. If you'd like me to represent him informally, your honor, I'll gladly do it.

JUDGE: Represent this beggar? Who'll take care of your fee?

PETER: I want to do it for the love of God. Let me try to question the poor lad, and see if I can't draw some relevant information out of him to rebut the accusation. He'll be in deep trouble if someone doesn't help him. *(To* TIB.*)* Come here, friend. Tell me all you know, all right?

TIB: Baa.

PETER: What do you mean, Baa? You're not crazy, I hope. Tell me the facts.

TIB: Baa.

PETER: Again? You're not in the meadows with your sheep. I'm trying to help you, don't you understand?

TIB: Baa.

PETER: Say yes or no. *(Low.)* Good work, keep it up. *(Loud.)* The facts!

TIB *(Softly.)*: Baa.

PETER: What was that? Louder, or you'll come to grief in this court!

TIB: Baa.

PETER: Well, it takes one madman to bring an action against another. Send him back to his sheep, your honor. He's a congenital idiot.

JOSS: Congenital hell! He's saner than you and me put together!

PETER: I repeat—send him back to his flock, and tell him not to show his face again in this courtroom. As for those, whoever they are, who drag these lunatics before the bar, they deserve a good flogging.

JOSS *(To the* JUDGE.*)*: Are you going to release him before hearing me out?

JUDGE: Why not, if he's crazy?
JOSS: I want to present my case. I have evidence, arguments, facts!
JUDGE: Oh God, more twaddle! I'm adjourning the court.
JOSS: Without making them come back?
JUDGE: How's that?
PETER: Come back! Don't bother answering him, your honor. They're both weak in the head. There's not an ounce of gray matter to be divided between them.
JOSS: Your scheme has succeeded, Mr. Quill; you've cheated me out of my cloth. But I tell you it isn't right, I'm a poor sinner, but it isn't just.
PETER: The man is daft.
JOSS: I know your voice, I know your dress, I know your face. I'm not daft, I can tell who treats me right and who treats me wrong. *(To the* JUDGE.*)* Your honor, I'll tell you my whole story from *A* to *Z*.
PETER: Not again! Your honor, tell him to stop. *(To* JOSS.*)* Aren't you ashamed to persecute this poor shepherd over three or four mangy sheep? Such a to-do—
JOSS: What sheep? I'm through with my sheep! I'm talking to you, and by Christ in the manger, you'll return my merchandise to me.
JUDGE: When is this fool going to stop yakking? Case dismissed!
JOSS: I demand—
PETER: Silence him, your honor, he's splitting our ears. *(To* JOSS.*)* Suppose he did knock down six, seven, or even a dozen of your beasts. Suppose he did eat them. So what? Has he ruined you? Are you in the poorhouse? You've earned a lot more than you've lost in all the years he's worked for you.
JOSS: Take note, your honor, I'm talking cloth and he's answering sheep. *(To* QUILL.*)* Where are my six yards, the six yards you stuck under your arm? Let me have them back!
PETER: Come now, Mr. Joss, I'm sure you don't want him to hang for six or seven woolbearing animals! Think again. Don't be so harsh with a poor and long-suffering shepherd who hasn't a suit on his back.

JOSS: That's not the question! The devil's in this! Your honor, I demand—
JUDGE: Case dismissed! Case dismissed! And I forbid you ever to proceed against this simpleton. *(To* TIB.*)* Go back to your sheep.
TIB: Baa.
JUDGE *(To* JOSS.*)*: As for you—
JOSS: My cloth! I've been swindled! Your honor, I must tell you—
JUDGE: This is a circus! I'm going home. *(To* TIB.*)* You're free, my lad, and don't ever come back. If anybody serves you a subpoena again, I squash it in advance. You're acquitted, understand?
PETER: Say thank you.
TIB: Baa.
JUDGE: Good enough.
JOSS: Is this justice?
JUDGE: I'm washing my hands of these jokers. Quill, come and dine with me, will you?
PETER: Another time, your honor.

(Exit the JUDGE.*)*

JOSS *(Aside.)*: Scoundrel! *(To* PETER.*)* Tell me now, are you or are you not going to pay me?
PETER: You've got a screw loose, my good man. I kept wondering all through the hearing, "Who does he take me for, anyway?"
JOSS: I'll be damned!
PETER: Maybe you took me for an ass. But I'd better warn you, I haven't brayed in many a year.
JOSS: Neither have I, and I'm telling you you're you. I'd know your voice anywhere.
PETER: You're telling me I'm me? Well, I'm not. Maybe you're confusing me with Rufus Pumpkin, we're about the same height.
JOSS: No, he doesn't have your drunkard's mug. Didn't I see you on your deathbed an hour ago?

PETER: Me? On my deathbed? Do I look sick? You've just proved that you're unbalanced.
JOSS: I have, have I? All right—I'm going straight to your house to look for you. We won't have to argue about it' here if I find you home.
PETER: Excellent idea. Go ahead and get it settled.

(Exit JOSS.)[2]

PETER: Well now, Tib, what do you say?
TIB: Baa.
PETER: Come on, how do you like the way I settled your business?
TIB: Baa.
PETER: Joss is gone. Don't bleat in my face. I hope you appreciate the way I tripped him up.
TIB: Baa.
PETER: Enough, Tib, enough, nobody can hear you. Don't be afraid to speak.
TIB: Baa.
PETER: As you wish. I'm on my way now, so let me have my fee.
TIB: Baa.
PETER: Actually, you gave a very neat performance. The trick depended on your keeping a straight face, and you certainly did.
TIB: Baa.
PETER: All right, all right! You can stop now. Kindly give me my money.
TIB: Baa.
PETER: May I say something? It's simply this. Be good enough to pay me without bleating my ears off. Money! Now!
TIB: Baa.
PETER: Better not try to pull my leg, Mr. Woolly. You'll pay me, do you hear, unless you learn how to fly. Come on—money!

[2] How will Peter Quill meet this new threat? Since the author provides no answer, it may be useful to give Quill an aside in performance; e.g., "Madge will know how to handle him."

TIB: Baa.
PETER: Money!
TIB: Baa.
PETER: Here I was so proud of you! Look at me, Tib, don't play games, let me be proud of you.
TIB: Baa.
PETER: God damn you! Have I lived to see a contemptible, half-naked two-legged goat get the better of me?
TIB: Baa.
PETER: I know it's all in fun, Tib, I'm not angry. Come along for a bite to eat at my house.
TIB: Baa.
PETER: You win. The mouse is chasing the cat. *(Aside.)* I thought I was the king of rogues, swindlers, sharpers, and schemers, but a simple shepherd has outwitted me. *(To* TIB.*)* I'll summon the police and have you arrested.
TIB: Baa.
PETER: Baa Baa! I'll be damned if I don't call a cop to throw you in the clink!
TIB *(Running away.)*: If he finds me, I'll forgive him!

THE END

TWO FARCES:

The Washtub

(LE CUVIER)

AND

The Chicken Pie and the Chocolate Cake

(LE PÂTÉ ET LA TARTE)

Authors Unknown

The comedy of *Pathelin* is too ambitious to serve as an example of the typical farce. Fortunately, several large French collections of brief farces have come down to us, along with a number of single texts. The two farces that follow were printed in this independent manner in the mid-sixteenth century, and then entered into a collection of sixty-four farces, *sotties*, and morality plays printed in the same period and surviving in a single copy discovered in an attic in Berlin around 1840. Both, however, have been authoritatively dated as late fifteenth-century plays.

The subjects are immemorial: the battle of the sexes; the mother-in-law; dousings and thrashings; hunger; thieving;

trickery; revenge; in a word, the *power play*—fundamental matter of the farce—which Strindberg was to turn into solemn drama centuries later, not at all to his advantage. In our own time, Albee, Strindberg's epigone, has also solemnized these conflicts, notably in *Who's Afraid of Virginia Woolf?* The humor he has added to his "tragic" struggle between husband and wife is far removed in its bitterness from the helter-skelter simplicities of the old farce. Yet a filiation exists. And what has happened is that middle-class and lower-class difficulties, once a terrain reserved to comedy, were gradually elevated by the advance of democracy to pathetic and tragic dignity. Only kings were entitled to tragedy once. Now you and I are. Hence the leap from *The Washtub* to *The Father*. That justice was the gainer is undeniable. That art was the loser is probable.

In *The Washtub* and *The Chicken Pie and the Chocolate Cake* we are, I think, justified in seeing the late descendants of the antique farces whose continued if unrecorded existence I have postulated throughout. I doubt that the fifteenth-century versions were far more sophisticated than the skits that must have been offered to the public delight five or ten centuries earlier. And I would also suggest that the puppet drama, which lives on solid drubbings, issued from farces like these, the second one especially.

Perhaps the puppet stage is more suitable nowadays for such farces than is the live theatre. We are always in danger of having our feelings of humanity interfere with our enjoyment of kicks and bruises. The puppet stage promptly sets up the unreality and distance that enable most of us to give satisfaction to the infantile brutality coiled in a corner of our minds. Unpestered by pity or fear, we guffaw at our ease over the absolutely primitive downfall of our fellow men and fellow women, whether or not they seem to deserve their fall. All downfalls are funny, provided pity and fear do not operate within us. But when the farce is staged by living performers, it may be that the civilized sector of our brain will send out disquieting messages: "the poor woman is suffering," or "the two tramps are hungry," or even "the social order is unjust, and the masters are pitiless." There are persons, all praise to them! who cannot bear the brutalities of the animated cartoon, which is nothing but farce in a modern guise.

The actors of the *commedia dell'arte* companies followed the Roman example by covering their faces with masks and their bodies with extraordinary costumes. Unconsciously they were transforming themselves into puppets, that is to say they were taking their stance outside of the too too solid flesh. And it is noteworthy that the two serious characters of the *commedia dell'arte*—the lovers, who did not get trounced or soaked—wore no masks: for them the mask, the distancing, was unnecessary.

Without masks, actors must still perform in such a way as to keep the door shut against pity and fear. The amateur will simply resort to wild exaggeration in motion and voice; the professional will exaggerate with art, and add elegance and acrobatic dexterity to his performance. We are helped, of course, by the fact that in the farce, as in the modern animated cartoon, the victim always bounces back. The broken bones are miraculously reset. This is the best trick of them all: The savage in us is satisfied because we witness a fall; the civilized mind is unruffled because the fall did not hurt.

I have used the texts in Barbara Bowen's *Four Farces* for these translations. Again I have modernized certain passages in accordance with the principles laid down in the general Introduction. For example, in the list of demands made by the wife in the first skit, the original bears an order to carry grain to the mill. I have replaced this and other tasks with modern chores. Timidity makes me keep the washtub, but in performance the whole action could easily be shifted to a riverbank. I need not insist that nothing archaic obtruded itself on the audience in either original. Nor anything merely odd; and for this reason I have changed the eel pie of *Le Pâté et la tarte* to the more familiar chicken pie. Both plays are in verse, but I have versified only the ending of each.

The staging of the second farce is much like that of *Peter Quill*. We see the street or road on one side, and a house with its interior on the other. The husband and wife are able to make an exit from the interior either to another room or to the street through the back and into the wings.

BIBLIOGRAPHY

FRANK, GRACE. *The Medieval French Drama.* Oxford, 1954, 1960. Chapter XXIV.

BOWEN, BARBARA C. (ed.). *Four Farces.* Oxford: Blackwell's French Texts, 1967. This has authoritative introductions and notes.

MAXWELL, IAN. *French Farce and John Heywood.* Melbourne, 1946.

THE WASHTUB

CHARACTERS

Jack
His wife
Her mother

JACK: It was the devil himself who made me get married. I've had nothing but tempests, storms, worry, and grief. My wife carries on like a beast, and her mother never fails to back her up. There's not a moment's peace, happiness, or relief for me. My brain feels as if pebbles were rolling around in it. The one yells, the other grumbles; one swears, the other rages at me. And that's the way I live weekdays and Sundays, with nothing else for entertainment. However, I swear by the blood of Christ who made me that I'll become master in my house the moment I make up my mind.
WIFE: Always complaining about something or other! If you know what's good for you, you'll keep your mouth shut.
MOTHER: What's the matter with him?
WIFE: How do I know? I have to mend whatever he touches, and besides he pays no attention to our household needs.
MOTHER: Why are you so unreasonable, Jack? My lord in heaven! A good husband ought to obey his wife. And if she decides to give you a hiding because you failed in your duties—
JACK: Ha! That'll be the day!
MOTHER: Why not? Goodness gracious! If she chastises you and tries to improve you now and then with a slap or two, do you think it's out of malice? Not in the least. A sign of love is what it is.
JACK: Very eloquent, mother dear. But why don't you tell me

in plain words what's on your mind instead of beating around the bush?

MOTHER: All I meant is—this is only your first year of marriage, dear mousy.

JACK: What's that? My name isn't mousy; it's Jack, and don't forget it.

MOTHER: Of course not, sweetheart. Jack the married man.

JACK: That I am; mauled and married.

MOTHER: Nonsense; you were never so well off.

JACK: Well off? I'll be damned! I'd be better off with my throat cut! Oh God! Well off!

MOTHER: Just listen to your wife whenever she gives you an order.

JACK: I get too many orders from her as it is; that's the very trouble.

MOTHER: Well, to keep them all in your head, you should make a list. Write all your duties down on a sheet of paper.

JACK: Why not? Go ahead. I'm writing.

WIFE: Write clearly, do you hear? Put down that you'll always obey me, never disobey me, and do everything I ask.

JACK: Nothing doing. Itemize, and I'll agree to what's reasonable.

WIFE: Let's get to the point. Put down, if you want to keep me happy, that you'll always get up first in the morning.

JACK: I object to that article! Get up first? What for?

WIFE: To warm my clothes by the fire.

JACK: Is that the custom?

WIFE: It is. Apparently you need a lesson in customs.

MOTHER: Write!

WIFE: Write, Jackie!

JACK: Don't rush me. I'm still at the first word.

WIFE: At night, if the baby wakes up—and he does all the time—it's your duty to get out of bed to rock him and carry him and walk him up and down the room no matter how late it is.

JACK: But that's not fair!

WIFE: Write!

THE WASHTUB 145

JACK: The sheet is full already. Where am I supposed to write?
WIFE: My palm is itching.
JACK: I guess there's room on the other side.
MOTHER: After that, Jackie boy, you'll have to run to the store for bread and milk.
WIFE: Also feed the cat, wash the clothes, and then hang them up to dry.
MOTHER: Come and go, hop, skip, and run, and sweat like Lucifer.
WIFE: Make the coffee.
MOTHER: Serve her breakfast.
WIFE: Then, to avoid a drubbing, make the bed.
MOTHER: Get lunch started and clean out the kitchen.
JACK: Wait, wait! If you want all this written down, you'll have to dictate word by word.
MOTHER: We don't mind. Let's start off: Buy the bread.
WIFE: And the milk.
MOTHER: Do the laundry.
WIFE: Make the coffee.
MOTHER: Serve her breakfast.
WIFE: Wash up.
JACK: Wash up what?
MOTHER: The pots and pans.
JACK: Slowly, slowly. Pots and pans.
WIFE: And all the dishes.
JACK: Damnation, I'm not bright enough to remember all this.
WIFE: Keep writing so you won't forget. Do you hear me? That's an order.
JACK: All right. Wash the—
WIFE: Baby's dirty diapers.
JACK: That does it! I won't put it down. Dirty diapers isn't decent.
WIFE: Put it down, ninny. What's there to be ashamed of?
JACK: I won't, I swear I won't.
WIFE: I can see I'll have to knock the lesson into your brain.
JACK: I'll put it down. Who am I to object? Forget I opened my mouth.

WIFE: The only item left is that you'll straighten out the house. And right now, quick as a rabbit, you'll help me wring the linen dry over the washtub.

JACK: It's all down.

MOTHER: One more article. Now and then you'll steal a moment to give her a bit of you know what.

JACK: I'll let her have a sample in two weeks or a month.

WIFE: Oh yes? Every day five or six times. At least! That's an order too.

JACK: I refuse, by the living God! Five or six times! All the saints help me! Neither five or six nor two or three. I'm not playing.

WIFE: Milksop, weakling, killjoy!

JACK: Jesus Christ, I'm an idiot to allow myself to be led by the nose. How can a man find a moment's rest in this house if he's kept busy with your list?

MOTHER: Don't forget the last article. Hurry up and sign.

JACK: Here, I've signed it. Keep it and don't lose it. From this moment on, I've sworn to do nothing except what's written down on that sheet, not even if it's to save myself from the hangman's noose.

MOTHER (*To the* WIFE.): Here, you keep it.

WIFE: Good-bye for now, mother dear.

(*The* MOTHER *leaves.*)

WIFE: On with the job. I want to see you sweat a little. Help me stretch these sheets out.[1] It's one of the articles in our contract.

JACK: What's that she's saying? I don't understand.

WIFE: I'll give you the back of my hand in a minute. I'm talking about the wash, you clown!

JACK: It's not in the list.

WIFE: It is too.

JACK: It's not.

---

[1] She stoops over the washtub and pulls out a wet sheet.

THE WASHTUB

WIFE: Oh no? Here it is, if you please. I hope it burns your hand.
JACK: All right, all right, I was wrong, it's in the list; I'll know better next time.
WIFE: There. Hold this end. Pull, pull hard.
JACK: God, is this sheet foul and smelly!
WIFE: The only foul thing around here is your mouth. Come on, do it nicely like me.
JACK: But it's disgusting I tell you! God what a household!
WIFE: I'll throw it all in your face, and don't think I'm joking.
JACK: No you won't, devils in hell.
WIFE: I won't? Here, fool.
JACK: Damnation, you've ruined my clothes!
WIFE: Nothing but alibis for not doing your work. Hold this end. And I hope you choke to death! *(She falls into the tub.)* Oh God, have mercy on me, look down on me, help me out of here or I'll die a shameful death! Jackie, save your wife! Pull her out of this tub!
JACK: It's not in the list.
WIFE: This tub is my death! Oh I'm so miserable! Help me out of here for God's sake!
JACK: Just turn up your backside, you drunken sack.
WIFE: Dearest, sweetest love, save my life! I'm dying. Give me your hand for one little second.
JACK: It's not in my list. Down to hell you go.
WIFE: Somebody help me before I drown!
JACK *(Reading from the list.)*: Buy the bread, make the coffee, serve breakfast, wash the pots and pans.
WIFE: I'm turning blue. I'm breathing my last.
JACK: Knock you up five times a day.
WIFE: Help. Help.
JACK: Come and go, hop, skip, and run.
WIFE: My last hour has struck.
JACK: Heat your clothes over the fire.
WIFE: Your hand, quick! This is the end.
JACK: Walk the baby.
WIFE: You're a dog.

JACK: Make up the bed in the morning.
WIFE: You think this is a laughing matter!
JACK: Hang up the laundry.
WIFE: Mother! Where's mother?
JACK: And keep the kitchen clean.
WIFE: Call a priest.
JACK: I'm scrutinizing this paper, but I have to inform you that it's not in the list.
WIFE: Why didn't you write it in?
JACK: Because you didn't make me. Save yourself any way you can. As far as I'm concerned you're staying where you are.
WIFE: At least go find a policeman to help me.[2]
JACK: It's not in the list.
WIFE: Won't you give me your hand, dearest? I'm ever so weak.
JACK: Dearest is it? I'm the enemy, drop dead!

(The MOTHER knocks at the door.)

MOTHER: Open up!
JACK: Who's knocking?
MOTHER: It's me. I've come to see how you are.
JACK: I'm fine, my wife is dead. Now I'm happy and rich.
MOTHER: What, my daughter is dead?
JACK: Drowned in the wash.
MOTHER: What's that? Murderer!
JACK: I pray to God in Paradise and their worships the saints in heaven to let the devil puncture her guts before the soul comes out.[3]
MOTHER: Is my daughter dead?
JACK: While she was wringing a sheet it fell out of her hands, she bent over the tub and fell in.
WIFE: Mother, I'm dead if you don't rescue your daughter.

[2] "Some servant or other in the street" is the original reading.
[3] In the absence of a stage direction, it may be more natural to keep the door between Jack and the Mother closed until this point.

MOTHER: Of course I will. Jack, give me a hand.
JACK: It's not in the list.
MOTHER: Is that a nice thing to say?
WIFE: Help!
MOTHER: Miserable cur, are you going to let her die?
JACK: As far as I'm concerned, yes. I don't want to be her flunky anymore.
WIFE: Help me.
JACK: It's not in the list. Can't find it anywhere.
MOTHER: Stop this nonsense at once, Jack, and help me get your wife out.
JACK: I swear I won't, unless I first receive a pledge that I'm to be master of the house.
WIFE: With all my heart, I promise, if only you'll pull me out of here.
JACK: And what do you promise to do?
WIFE: I'll do all the chores, I'll never bother you, and never give you an order unless it's absolutely necessary.
JACK: That's good. Now I'll pull you out. But you'd better keep your promise, by God.
WIFE: I will, and I'll never break it, dear.
JACK: Well then, it looks as if I'll be in charge from now on, since my wife says so.

MOTHER: A rotten business is strife
Between husband and his wife.

JACK: Then let the world be told
A wife should never scold
Nor make her man a slave
Though he be fool or knave.

WIFE: I've learned my lesson too.
I'll never be a shrew.
With diligence and zeal
On my two knees I'll kneel
To scrape and scrub the floor
Under the husband I adore.
Because the rule must be obeyed:
He's my master, I'm his maid.

JACK: Always please me, always mind me,
Always walk two steps behind me,
And I will love you, sweet,
Provided you don't cheat.
From this day on I'll live in clover.
Adieu, my friends, the play is over.

THE END

THE CHICKEN PIE
AND THE CHOCOLATE CAKE

CHARACTERS

First Rogue
Second Rogue
Husband, a pastrycook
His wife

Street.

FIRST ROGUE: Ay ay ay!
SECOND ROGUE: What's the matter?
FIRST ROGUE: I'm cold, I'm shivering, and I've got nothing but rags over my skin.
SECOND ROGUE: It's a rough time for both of us. Ay ay ay!
FIRST ROGUE: What's the matter?
SECOND ROGUE: I'm cold, I'm shivering.
FIRST ROGUE: Poor beggars are out of luck nowadays. Ay ay ay!
SECOND ROGUE: What's the matter?
FIRST ROGUE: I'm cold, I'm shivering, I'm dressed in rags and shreds.[1]
SECOND ROGUE: What about me?
FIRST ROGUE: I'm worse off than you, because I'm famished and penniless.
SECOND ROGUE: Couldn't you find a way of getting a bite to eat?
FIRST ROGUE: Let's stretch out our hands from door to door.
SECOND ROGUE: We'd better take separate ways, don't you think?

---

[1] A number of farces use this technique of singsong refrains.

FIRST ROGUE: If you say so. But we'll share and share alike, all right? Whether it's meat or bread or butter or eggs.
SECOND ROGUE: Certainly. Shall we start?

House.

HUSBAND: Mary!
WIFE: What is it, Walt?
HUSBAND: I'm dining in town with friends. There's a chicken pie on the table that I want you to send me when I call for it.
WIFE: I will, dear.

Street.

FIRST ROGUE: Hey, this sounds like a good deal. Let's start here.
SECOND ROGUE: One of us is enough. I'll go scouting my way and you see what you can grab here. All right?
FIRST ROGUE: All right.

(Exit SECOND ROGUE.*)*

FIRST ROGUE *(Knocking at the door.)*: May the saints rain blessings on your house. Charity for the poor.
WIFE *(At the door.)*: There's nobody in the house just now, my good man. Come back another time.

Inside.

HUSBAND: While I'm thinking about the pie, don't hand it over to anybody unless he gives you a sure sign.
WIFE: Don't worry. I won't give it away if I'm suspicious of the messenger.
HUSBAND: The man I send you will take your little finger like this. Get it?
WIFE: Oh yes.

(Exit the HUSBAND.*)*

THE CHICKEN PIE AND THE CHOCOLATE CAKE 153

FIRST ROGUE: Am I glad I overheard their conversation! *(He knocks again.)* Merciful lady, won't you take pity on me? I haven't had a crumb to eat in two and a half days.
WIFE: Ask God to help you. *(She goes back inside.)*
FIRST ROGUE: God strike you deaf and dumb!

(Enter the SECOND ROGUE.)

SECOND ROGUE: I'm as hungry as ever and I don't see my pal. I won't stand for it if he tries to cheat me out of my half. Oh, there he is. Any success?
FIRST ROGUE: No success, and I'm fighting mad besides. How about you?
SECOND ROGUE: I couldn't squeeze a nickel out of anybody, as God is my witness.
FIRST ROGUE: Some dinner we're going to have today!
SECOND ROGUE: Can't you think of a trick to find us something to eat?
FIRST ROGUE: I can, if you'll go where I tell you.
SECOND ROGUE: I'm your friend for life! Tell me where.
FIRST ROGUE: Go to the pastrycook's house over there, and ask for a chicken pie. Don't forget to act sure of yourself. Take the wife's little finger like this and tell her, "Your husband wants you to give me this chicken pie." All right?
SECOND ROGUE: But supposing he's come back already? How will I talk my way out?
FIRST ROGUE: I know he hasn't come back, because he left a minute ago.
SECOND ROGUE: Take her finger, eh? All right, here I go. *(He hesitates.)*
FIRST ROGUE: Go on, you blockhead.
SECOND ROGUE: Damn it, I don't want to get walloped if he's there after all.
FIRST ROGUE: Nothing ventured, nothing gained.
SECOND ROGUE: You're right. Off I go. *(He knocks at the door.)* Lady, your husband wants you to send him that chicken pie. How about it?
WIFE: What's the sign, my friend?

SECOND ROGUE: He told me to take your little finger. Give me your hand.
WIFE: That's the sign sure enough. Here's the pie.
SECOND ROGUE: I'll take it to him right away. (*The* WIFE *re-enters the house.*) I've got it! I've got it! What a brain, what genius! Look at it!
FIRST ROGUE: You got the pie?
SECOND ROGUE: Didn't I though! Didn't I though! What do you say?
FIRST ROGUE: You're brilliant. Three could make a feast with this pie!

(*Exeunt the* TWO ROGUES. *Enter the* HUSBAND.)

HUSBAND: Well, they've stood me up, the jokers, and I'm an ass to have waited so long. Damn them. I'll go eat that chicken pie with my wife. If there's anything I hate, it's being made a fool of. I'm back, Mary! (*He enters the house.*)
WIFE: My goodness, did you have your dinner?
HUSBAND: No I didn't, and I'm mad as a wasp. Devil hang them!
WIFE: But then why did you send for the pie, you dummy?
HUSBAND: Who sent?
WIFE: Listen to the man playing dumb!
HUSBAND: What playing dumb? Wait a minute. Don't tell me you gave it to somebody!
WIFE: Of course I did. A man came to the house, took me by the finger, and told me to hand over the pie.
HUSBAND: How hand over? God damn it to hell, is my pie gone?
WIFE: For goodness' sake, it's you who sent for it, with the sign and all.
HUSBAND: You're a liar! I didn't send for it! What did you do with it?
WIFE: That's a good one! I'm telling you, I gave it to the man who came for it a little while ago.
HUSBAND: Fire and brimstone! I need my stick. You ate it!
WIFE: Stop babbling. I gave it to the man you sent.
HUSBAND: You'll pay for this. I won't take it lying down. You ate it!

THE CHICKEN PIE AND THE CHOCOLATE CAKE 155

WIFE: Now I'm beginning to see red.

HUSBAND: Where's that stick? Wait till I tickle your back with it. The truth! What did you do with the chicken pie? *(He whacks her.)*

WIFE: Murder! He's murdering me! You louse, you tramp!

HUSBAND: Where's that pie? I'll knock the stuffings out of you. Did you eat it without me? Where's that pie?

WIFE: Murder! He's murdering me! I gave it to the man you sent with the sign!

HUSBAND: I'm bursting with anger, I'm starved, and there's nothing left to eat!

(Exeunt HUSBAND and WIFE. Enter the TWO ROGUES.)

FIRST ROGUE: What do you say?

SECOND ROGUE: The pie was scrumptious. Now if you wanted to do your bit, we could get our hands on a beautiful chocolate cake I saw in the house.

FIRST ROGUE: Why don't you go yourself? Take the woman's finger again and tell her that her husband sent for the cake.

SECOND ROGUE: Don't talk nonsense. I've done my share of the work. Now it's your turn.

FIRST ROGUE: All right, I'll go, but keep my half of what's left of the pie.

SECOND ROGUE: Who do you take me for? What's yours is yours, and I swear nobody's going to touch this till you return.

FIRST ROGUE: You're a real pal. Well, I'm off. Wait for me here.

In the house.

WIFE: You've beaten me black and blue. Damn that chicken pie.

HUSBAND: I gave your bones a lesson they needed. Enough. I'm off to cut some wood in the shed.

WIFE: The quicker the better.

(Exit the HUSBAND. The FIRST ROGUE knocks at the door.)

FIRST ROGUE: Lady! Your husband has sent me for the chocolate cake. He's fit to be tied because you didn't send it along with the chicken pie.
WIFE: Oh, I'm glad you came. Please step inside.

(The HUSBAND pops in.)

HUSBAND: So you're the rascal! Oh I'm going to cuddle you. *(Beating him.)* What did you do with the pie you picked up here?
FIRST ROGUE: Ay ay ay, it wasn't me!
HUSBAND: What did you do with my pie? I'll beat you into the ground!
FIRST ROGUE: Murder!
HUSBAND: What did you do with my pie?
FIRST ROGUE: I'll tell you the whole story if you'll stop hitting me!
HUSBAND: Talk, you rascal, or I'll knock you to kingdom come.
FIRST ROGUE: I'm talking, I'm talking. A while ago I came here to beg, but nobody gave me a penny. Then I overheard you telling your wife about the pie and giving her the sign. My dear kind sir, I was ravenous, so I went back to my buddy who's as sharp as a razor blade. We're loyal to each other, share and share alike, half his, half mine, whatever we earn. I told him about the sign of the little finger, he came here for the pie, and believe me I'm sorry he ever did. After we'd eaten it the devil reminded him there was a cake here too. Then like a fool I walked in to ask for it.
HUSBAND: Now, by God, I'll beat your brains out if you don't swear to make your friend come to me for his share of the cake. Since you split everything between you, he's got a right to the same treat you had.
FIRST ROGUE: I swear I'll send him to you. And be sure to make him feel the end of your stick.
HUSBAND: On your way, and play it natural.
FIRST ROGUE: As God is my witness he'll get what I got. *(He joins the SECOND ROGUE.)*
SECOND ROGUE: How's that? You came back empty-handed?

THE CHICKEN PIE AND THE CHOCOLATE CAKE 157

FIRST ROGUE: Listen, she cut me short and told me she'd give the cake to nobody but the man who came for the pie.
SECOND ROGUE: I'll go right away. God, I can taste it already! Watch me do my ploy. *(He goes to the house.)* Hey there!
WIFE: Who is it?
SECOND ROGUE: Lady, let me have the chocolate cake for your husband.
WIFE: Dear me! Come in!

(The HUSBAND *jumps out.)*

HUSBAND: Thief! Traitor! I'll fix you up for the hangman. There, there, there, a hundred knocks for the chicken pie.
SECOND ROGUE: Mercy, mercy!
WIFE: Thump him a hundred times! How does it feel! Because of you I was thrashed till my bones ached.
HUSBAND: One hundred knocks. There, there, there's for the chicken pie.
SECOND ROGUE: Have mercy on me! I'll never do it again! I'm crippled for life! I'm dead!
WIFE: Harder, Walt, harder, let him remember the pie.
HUSBAND: Go to hell now, and I hope somebody wraps your gut around your neck.

(Exeunt HUSBAND *and* WIFE. *The* SECOND ROGUE *joins the first.)*

SECOND ROGUE: You double-crossing bastard, you sent me off to be murdered!
FIRST ROGUE: Aren't we supposed to share and share alike, the good as well as the bad? What do you say, you dumb ape? He hit me ten times worse than you.
SECOND ROGUE: If only you'd warned me, I would never have gone. Oh Jesus, I'm one big sore.
FIRST ROGUE: You know what they say—one rogue shouldn't trust another.
SECOND ROGUE: Never mind. Let's finish the pie and forget about the cake. We can still stuff ourselves.
    What are we, me and you?
    Robbers beaten black and blue.

FIRST ROGUE:
>Though you're right, you needn't shout;
>It's not a thing I'd boast about.
>Let's take our aching spines away,
>And hope the audience liked our play.

THE END